P9-CRF-714

THE
WELL
FUL
NESS
PROJECT

ALI ROFF FARRAR

THE WELL FUL NESS PROJECT

A manual for mindful living

aster

An Hachette UK Company
www.hachette.co.uk
First published in Great Britain in 2020
by Aster, an imprint of Octopus Publishing
Group Ltd, Carmelite House, 50 Victoria
Embankment, London EC4Y 0DZ

www.octopusbooks.co.uk

Text copyright © Ali Roff Farrar 2020
Design and layout copyright © Octopus
Publishing Group 2020

Distributed in the US by Hachette Book Group
1290 Avenue of the Americas
4th and 5th Floors, New York, NY 10104

Distributed in Canada by
Canadian Manda Group
664 Annette St, Toronto, Ontario,
Canada M6S 2C8

All rights reserved. No part of this work may be
reproduced or utilized in any form or by any
means, electronic or mechanical, including
photocopying, recording or by any information
storage and retrieval system, without the prior
written permission of the publisher.

Ali Roff Farrar asserts the moral right to be
identified as the author of this work.

ISBN 978-1-78325-321-0

A CIP catalogue record for this book is available
from the British Library.

Printed and bound in China

10 9 8 7 6 5 4 3 2 1

Publishing Director: Stephanie Jackson
Art Director: Yasia Williams
Senior Editor: Sophie Elletson
Design & Illustration: Nicky Collings
& Aaron Blecha
Production Manager: Lisa Pinnell

To unconditional love.
Mine, yours, ours.

Contents

Well-ful-ness

noun.

the quality or state of combining ancient
wisdom with contemporary psychology to
create life-enhancing transformation through
greater awareness.

MY STORY

In my early twenties, I was constantly dieting for the sole purpose of being fashionably thin. I was binge exercising and living for the weekend to escape from my boredom at work. I was desperately unhappy and constantly comparing myself to others. I was tired, bored, stressed and unhealthy in my body, my mind and my heart. I was living in reaction to my life, rather than in response to it.

But I've discovered that health is a holistic, all-encompassing globe that lights up only when all areas of it are linked as a whole. If one area is left unnurtured, the other areas cannot thrive. When I ate without attention, my stomach would bloat. When my emotional world was turned upside down, my skin would break out in spots. When I drank mindlessly, my success was stifled. It was only when I looked at my life with mindful curiosity that I became aware of how the things I was doing were making me feel. This, in turn, helped me to find the kindness and courage in myself to change what I could and accept what I couldn't.

The way I live my life has become more conscious. I notice and examine life more closely and get interested in it. It's a very small shift that, with practice, has become a part of the way I think – and it's changed everything. Since practising Wellfulness in my own life, I am more confident and I have a healthier body image. I'm more successful – I have my dream job, I'm my own boss and run a thriving retreat company. I have better friendships, a stronger marriage. I have more positivity in my life, less gossiping, fewer toxic people. I eat in accordance with my body's needs and my heart's values. I work out because I want to, not because I have to, and I have a more stable and healthier weight – no more yo-yoing. I'm fitter and stronger, and I can do things with my body I'd only ever thought gymnasts could – this year I cracked the elusive handstand in my yoga practice. I'm happier, more peaceful, and I react less and respond more when things in life get tough. I know my values and I live to them. I understand myself. I am my own guide.

Through Wellfulness, I want to empower you to discover your own individual wellness practices that work for you and your unique needs – to inspire you to look within and be your own guide. I want you to take back ownership of your body, mind and heart, and ultimately your health – both mental and physical. It's yours, and always has been yours. All it takes is a little mindful curiosity...

Making a change

You're holding this book, so you're probably interested in making some kind of change in your life. You might want a healthier body that you feel more comfortable or confident in. You might want to create a more holistic and healthy lifestyle. You might want to make your life more authentic to you and your needs. Or you might not know what needs to change, only that something does.

Maybe you have some practices in your life that enhance your holistic health already – a fridge stocked with fresh veg, a regular yoga class, gym membership and perhaps even a committed meditation practice. You might take vitamin supplements, try to use natural products as much as possible, or make sure you get a daily walk. Wellness looks different for everyone, and so it should. We all have unique body types, personalities, likes, interests and needs. But in a world of information overload, it can often feel confusing to know which trend or piece of new research to follow and, so often, just when you think you have it figured out, someone tells you, 'Actually, there's some new research that says…'

Take food as an example. My mother was told that fat was 'evil' and turned to products that were low in fat (yet often unknowingly pumped with sugar to replace the loss of flavour) in order to live a healthier lifestyle. Today, researchers tell us that, actually, fat is not our main enemy, but sugar is the poison to avoid. And what about all the diet trends that are available for us to follow when it comes to what we eat?

- [ ] Atkins or Paleo?
- [ ] FODMAP or macros?
- [ ] Plant-based, vegan or fruitarian?

I even met a person on retreat in Ibiza who only ate bananas – 21 a day, to be precise!

So just choosing what to eat can sometimes feel like a minefield. It is not surprising that many of us find ourselves at the end of a long day at work, aimlessly looking into the fridge with decision fatigue.

Then there's the endless stream of advice on every other area of healthy living.

- HIIT or yoga?
- The KonMari Method or Swedish Death Cleaning?
- 'How to be more productive', or 'the lost art of wasting time'?

You may be beginning to feel that wellness and self-development is a never-ending to-do list, which only adds to feeling overwhelmed in your already busy life. Or, worst-case scenario, that you're bringing wellness practices into your life because you feel you 'should', rather than because they truly serve you.

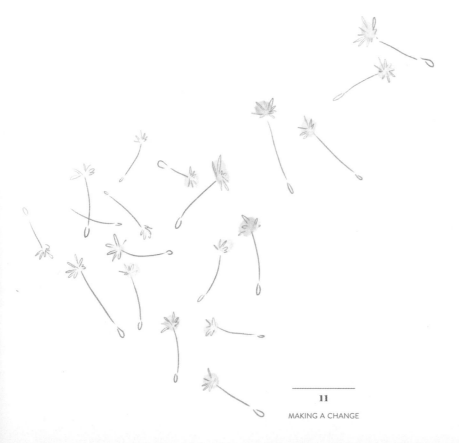

We are all unique

We are all different. What works for me and my body, might not work for you. Each one of us has a different body shape, skeletal structure and metabolic rate. Also, we all have different skills and things we're naturally good at. You might, for example, have long, powerful legs and be a fast runner, while your shorter-legged friend cannot move as quickly but is more flexible and finds yoga postures easier to do than you. And, most importantly, we all have different likes, dislikes, interests, passions and things that make us feel great and make our hearts sing. Despite your long, powerful legs, you might find running tedious, but love yoga – even if you find it difficult. And these unique distinctions can be found in every element of our lives. For example, you might feel passionately about protecting the environment, while your friend is more interested in preparing healthy food.

When it comes to our physical bodies, interests of the mind and passions of the heart, we don't live in a one-size-fits-all world. To create a lifestyle that suits our own unique health and wellness needs, and fits into our busy lives, we must find the practices that are authentic to our own body's requirements, our mind's distinctive interests and our heart's values and passions.

But with all the 'expert' tips from friends, articles in magazines and personal development and wellness books advising us on what to do, how do we find what will work for us and create real results? And how do we find what is authentic for us, so that our healthy lifestyles become sustainable, and even enjoyable?

How to use this book

The Wellfulness Project can be used alone and as a manual by itself, or alongside any other wellness book or concept you're following; from fitness and nutrition, to meditation and yoga, self-help/development and even interiors/space. It's designed to sit alongside any other wellness idea, practice or trend you either currently practice, or decide to embrace either now or in the future, to help you discover whether it is serving you. I hope that this will be a book you refer back to throughout your life, and that the practices and tools within it habitually become a part of your day, every day.

The first time you read this book, try to follow the order the chapters are set out in, as you'll get more out of the process if you build your awareness from the outside in. After you've laid the foundations and completed the project once (or as many times as you like), you can come back to the book at any point to work on a specific area.

ARE WE REPLACING OUR INNER WISDOM?

There is the part of ourselves where our inner wisdom lives. I like to call it my heartspace. You might call it your gut, your spirit or your soul. Maybe the idea of having an 'inner guide' resonates with you. But we are often so absorbed by our smartphones today, never finding time for that life-changing study of tuning in to the inner workings of our minds. We fill nearly all our empty moments – waiting for the bus, or during the adverts between TV programmes or even just walking down the street – entertaining ourselves with the apps and websites that live in our pockets. Apparently, around 80 per cent of us have felt phantom vibrations from our phones, only to pick them up and realize that no one has left a message or called – no one loves us! Are we becoming so used to the 'ping' or a vibration from our smartphones, that we've learned to tune into the technology in our pockets over the subtler signals coming from our bodies? Is the omnipresent Google search in our pocket replacing our inner 'gut' wisdom?

Part One
Introducing Wellfulness

'Your mind, this globe
of awareness, is a starry
universe. When you push off
with your foot, a thousand
new roads become clear.'

— Rumi

TAKING BACK OWNERSHIP

I've always been drawn to places where the ocean meets the land. Sometimes there is a soft, peaceful kneading of waves on the sand, at other times a great theatrical surge of powerful spray. As I discovered mindfulness, I began to play around with bringing the 'meditation' of mindful awareness to my daily life and found that this would be particularly fun to do when near the ocean – giving my attention to the magic of the shoreline, as I explored every sound, smell and sensation, even the way it made me feel emotionally. Nature has a way of allowing us to move more quickly into our internal experience. Most of us have felt moved by nature at some point in our lives, whether by a beautiful sunset, the birdsong on a summer's morning, or in voyeuristic awe of an other-worldly landscape on a television documentary or film.

As I spent time mindfully watching the ocean, I noticed that the shorelines were ever-changing; the water, sometimes peaceful, sometimes wild, was transient, just like the world I lived in and the emotions I felt. And then mindfulness gave me another gift – the gift of curiosity.

One day, as I walked and watched the shore with mindful inquisitiveness, observing the water gather up and roll in towards the land – noting every crash of a wave, the spray bounce off the rocks and the rebound of water back into the ocean – I realized with curiosity that this thing that I had seen as a beautiful and harmonious dance between water and land is, if you look a little closer, in fact a battle. The waves covet the land, relentlessly trying to claim and eat it up, and the land, resilient and determined, pushes the water back with stoic force. All this was no less beautiful to me, but from a place of curiosity I had experienced it differently than I had from a place of simple observation. I had found its truth.

So often we take the world as it has always been presented to us – seeing it one way and never looking any deeper, never looking at it again with curious eyes. That experience prompted me to ask, what else in my life do I take simply as it has been given to me? What else could I apply more mindful curiosity to, in order to find truth? And how could this truth change my life? As it turns out, it had the power to change everything.

What is mindfulness?

Mindfulness is one of those things that you can't really explain. I can use words to describe mindfulness, but in my experience, mindfulness needs to be felt to be understood fully. It is your own lived experience of it that has the greatest impact; that's where the real magic and understanding is to be found. And that's what I hope you will find in this book.

There has been a huge amount of research on the benefits of mindfulness on both mental and physical health, resulting in some serious scientific evidence to show how it works. The conclusions of these studies can seem too good to be true – from showing that just 25 minutes of mindfulness meditation for 3 consecutive days has the power to alleviate psychological stress, to finding that partaking in an 8-week mindfulness meditation course has the power to create significant change in the brain's grey matter, specifically in the areas associated with memory, sense of self and stress.

I've had the privilege of interviewing mindfulness experts such as Deepak Chopra, Ed Halliwell, Tamara Russell and Jon Kabat-Zinn, the man who brought mindfulness to the West and created a secular, stress-reducing offering of it from its Buddhist roots. Talking to these experts and reporting on their compelling research led me to start practising mindfulness myself.

I found the evidence around the benefits of mindfulness so undeniable, it seemed a no-brainer that I needed it in my life. I started with basic meditations and mindful practices, such as taking moments to focus on the sounds of birds in the trees or to watch the steam rise from a cup of hot tea. I fell in love with the way practising compassion towards myself and others felt in my heart and, very quickly, I began to feel the benefits of mindfulness for myself. As the months and years went by, my personal transformation through mindfulness led me to study and teach it. It brings me great joy to see others grasp and transform their own lives through this beautiful practice.

GAINING ANCIENT WISDOM

Many of the ideas, concepts and practices in this book stem from yogic and other ancient Eastern philosophies. Most of these ideas and thoughts were born in the Indus Valley, around 15,000–500 BCE, a time of sages, seekers and seers, who would take themselves to remote places, such as in the desert or up high mountains, to meditate and contemplate their thoughts. As trade routes – known as the Silk Road – opened, ideas, stories and philosophies were also shared.

In this way, concepts crossed over and often mingled seamlessly – the Four Noble Truths of Buddhism, for example, align beautifully with *The Yoga Sutras of Patanjali*. Essentially, they both look at the roots of suffering, the ill health of body and mind, and ways in which to heal and prevent it. At the heart of all of these ancient teachings is union – we are all one and all seeking freer, fuller lives.

You'll notice I use the term 'yogic philosophy' a lot, and I also use some Zen stories that have been imparted to me by my own teachers. As you work through the book, you might start to wonder how religion fits into it. It's true that when we start thinking about 'ancient Eastern wisdom' and religion it can get a bit confusing to say the least! If you do identify with a religion, please feel soothed that this book, and the teachings it takes from ancient Eastern wisdoms, isn't about religion. In fact, yogic philosophy predates most organized religion – the first of the yogic scriptures were written 900–500 BCE, which also predates the physical practice of yoga as we know it in the West.

The mindfulness myth

You may have heard mindfulness described as 'being in the moment'. But that's only the beginning. Hearing the birds in the trees or watching steam rise from hot tea – in other words, finding awareness of the present moment *outside* of yourself – is simply where you lay the foundations. Living 'in the moment' is a brilliant tool to help you move away from a constant state of worrying about the future or regretting the past. It gives you a chance to enjoy the only reality there ever is – now. But it is just the first step. When you use the present moment as a launch pad to move into a deeper, more meaningful practice of mindfulness – this is when true transformation happens.

By practising mindfulness, you start to carve new neural grooves in your brain – clearing pathways in the metaphorical forest of your mind that allow you to live more easily in the present. Old neural pathways from worrying about the future or the past may have been well-trodden, but as you use them less and less through your mindfulness practice, and take the 'path of the present moment' more and more frequently, you'll find you have more awareness or more choice in your life. This is what a daily mindfulness practice will cultivate – you will literally be reshaping the structure of your brain to be more aware of the present moment. You will learn to be an observer of your thoughts about the future or the past, instead of living inside them.

How? To help us begin to find awareness in the present moment, we ground ourselves in the direct experiences happening outside of ourselves. It's easier to bring our focus to these external experiences, because we are usually unattached to them, so they are comfortable for us to sit with. But we are using our focus on these external experiences as training for the *real* thing, because the true magic and transformation through mindfulness is found when we begin to look within and become aware of how we feel *inside* our bodies, minds and hearts, and of the judgements, preferences and stories that are attached to those feelings. We identify our *samskaras* – our habitual patterns – the things we do without real question, and from there are able to gain clarity around what they truly do for us – whether they serve or not – and then we can make change.

Many elements of mindfulness are also found in yoga – in TKV Desikachar's classic yoga text, *The Heart of Yoga*, he describes one style of yoga – *kriya* yoga – as 'attentiveness in action'. It can be easy to think that awareness is passive, a simple observation of our lives with no action involved, but awareness around what we do with our observations is just as important.

Mindful empowerment

For me, mindfulness is at the core of understanding and creating holistic wellness, be it within food, movement, habits, rituals, values, mindset, spaces or relationships. Through the practice of mindful awareness, we can introduce conscious change and conscious acceptance into our lives in order to find a more harmonious and authentic relationship with our wellbeing.

By creating an awareness around how our wellness practices make us feel, firstly, we find the space to create real change in our lives and in our health – physically and mentally. But we can also use our wellness practices as a channel to access a deeper practice of mindfulness – to look inside ourselves in order to become truly aware and conscious – and to live with a greater sense of peace, happiness and understanding.

✓ *Mindfulness*:
non-judgemental awareness + kindness and compassion = acceptance

What is Conscious Awareness?

In an age of social media, where everyone's got a life-changing piece of wisdom to share, I think it's my duty before we begin our journey together, to mention that nobody is perfect. Even during the process of writing this book, when you'd think I would have been my most mindful self, I had moments of reaction rather than response. I had periods of feeling chronically stressed, to the point that I had to go for emergency acupuncture before I came apart at the seams. And, on several occasions, I definitely ate more chocolate biscuits in a day than are generally considered healthy! And that's OK. We are not here to be perfect. I don't always manage to meditate for an hour every single day; I don't know one person who does – who isn't a Buddhist monk! I don't always choose healthy options every time I eat – that's not realistic either. I've found that when we try to follow plans or goals too rigidly, and are not authentic to ourselves, we only set ourselves up for failure.

What I do hold myself accountable for every day, however, is to practise conscious awareness around the choices I make. If I eat one too many chocolate biscuits, I am aware, honest, non-judgemental and kind with myself about how it makes me feel. If I skip the gym because I'm feeling lazy, not in my body but in my mind, again, all I ask of myself is mindful, non-judgemental awareness of how that feels in my body, mind and heart. If I don't have time to meditate, I am simply aware, honest and mindful about how that makes me feel. That's real mindfulness. That's real spirituality. No one is perfect, not me, not you, not your favourite guru or influencer, and that in itself is something to practise awareness around. So, let's be kind to ourselves and remember that even our perceived failures, slip-ups, imperfections, flaws or unhealthy habits, are not only perfect opportunities to be mindful around, but also fertile ground from which to create real transformation in our lives.

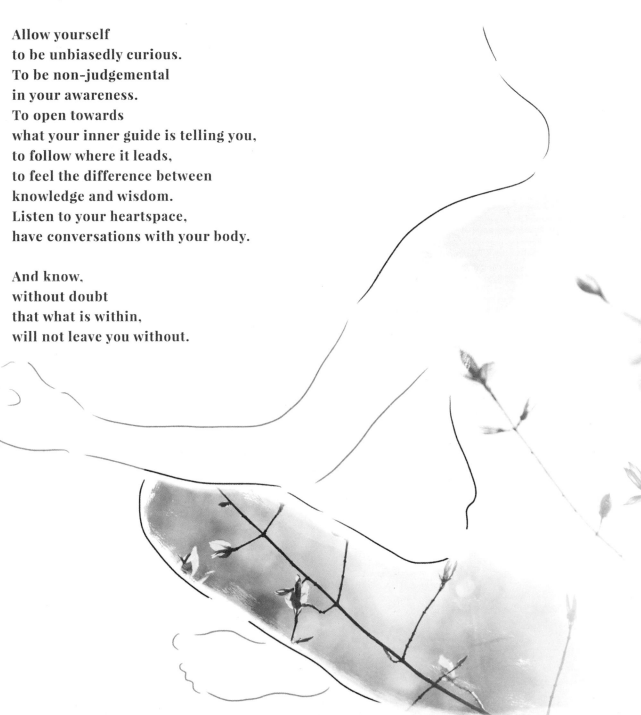

Wellful

Allow yourself
to be unbiasedly curious.
To be non-judgemental
in your awareness.
To open towards
what your inner guide is telling you,
to follow where it leads,
to feel the difference between
knowledge and wisdom.
Listen to your heartspace,
have conversations with your body.

And know,
without doubt
that what is within,
will not leave you without.

What is Wellfulness?

To me, the concept of Wellfulness means using mindful awareness to create greater wellness in body and mind. Wellfulness is more than simple awareness – it is awareness combined with conscious, attentive action, which has the power to create changes for the better in all areas of our lives. Yes, we have this wealth of information at our fingertips when it comes to how to live a happy, healthy lifestyle in both body and mind. But we must first identify the concepts and practices that work for us within that world of information.

With this book, I want to empower you to create a wellness plan that actually works for you, one that is adaptable as your needs and interests change over a lifetime and one that is easy to follow because it's authentic to your interests, likes and passions. I want to help you to create a holistically healthy lifestyle that is second nature to you, that fits into the natural rhythm of your life and feels a part of who you are. And the first key to knowing how to do this is differentiating between the knowledge that you can gather on how to be healthy and the wisdom within you that helps you judge what to do with that knowledge, rather than simply following it.

I know what it's like to want to be healthier, but feel that's just another thing on the to-do list. I know what it is to feel overwhelmed with options on how to bring wellness into your life or to fit into a specific version of a healthy lifestyle, rather than having a healthy lifestyle that fits *you*.

So, I'll invite you at this point to take a breath, close your eyes and feel your feet on the earth. Notice the gentle, grounding force of gravity rooting you to the spot. Feel the weight of this book in your hands. Breathe three, deep, long breaths, then open your eyes and come back to the page.

'Knowledge is knowing that a tomato is a fruit. Wisdom is knowing not to put it in a fruit salad.'

- Miles Kington

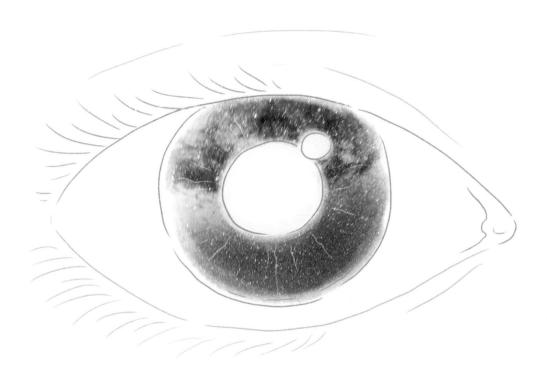

I have an academic background in the Western science of psychology and, more recently, have studied the Eastern practices of yoga and mindfulness (which is rooted in Buddhism). I love to bring the two together, as they complement each other beautifully in so many areas and also serve a purpose in helping to understand the difference between knowledge and wisdom.

Western science needs studies, evidence and facts – it is knowledge-based; the ancient Eastern philosophies are based on intuition and deep inner wisdom. Both are so very useful in our world, but modern society largely champions knowledge-based information, which can take us away from our intuitive wisdom. If we are ill, we're taught to go to a doctor and ask to be cured. If we feel sadness, we're advised to go to a certified counsellor for help. And of course, all of these experts have an important part to play in keeping us healthy, but to always depend on others when we need help, or to be fixed, or soothed or told what to do, takes away agency over our own bodies, minds and lives.

What if we could depend on our own inner wisdom more, to know what we need intuitively? We will always need professional healers, but I believe we owe it to ourselves to champion our own inner wisdom over our bodies and minds, first and foremost. Our lives are busy and there is more information about health and wellness out there than ever. But in order to navigate through it, we must find a sense of conscious awareness around what we're choosing to bring into our lives, and why. To create a healthy and happy life that's authentic to us, we must check out of our 'knowledge mindset' and check into our 'wisdom mindset'.

Discovering what nourishes you

By using Wellfulness, you can begin to cultivate the awareness you need to put together a specific blueprint of practices for your holistic health that is uniquely created by you, for you.

Together, we will navigate through each wellness idea or practice in your life and use the information gathered to connect on a deep level with what your body, mind and heart is telling you about it, by bringing awareness to how the idea or practice makes you feel. Through deep awareness, Wellfulness allows you to determine what serves you, nourishes you and improves your life – or identify what's falling flat, makes little or no difference and wastes your time, energy or money. You can then make a conscious choice around whether you want to hold on to an idea or practice, or let it go.

Using awareness to create change isn't a new concept, or one that's been thought up as a gimmicky mindfulness practice, rather one that has been forgotten. In the ancient yogic text, *The Yoga Sutras of Patanjali*, a compilation of aphorisms (put together prior to 400CE no less!), it states, 'through focusing our attention onto our habits and conditioning, we gain knowledge and understanding of our past and of how we can change the habitual patterns that aren't serving us in order to live more freely and fully.' This is the key. To enhance your life – whether that may be having a healthier body, or a more harmonious physical space to spend time in, or more enjoyable work, or less toxic relationships or a quieter mind – you must look within and observe the things you do in your day-to-day life.

Part Two
Starting Your
Wellfulness Journey

'Study thy self,
discover the divine.'

- the Yoga Sutras
of Patanjali.

II.44

LOOKING WITHIN

I have touched upon Patanjali's sutra that looks at reasons for creating a more conscious space around our behaviour and habits – 'to live more freely and fully' (see page 19). For me, when I think about why I want to invest in my holistic wellness, this resonates on a deep level. When I ask myself why I want to live healthily, ultimately it is because I want to live *free* of physical and emotional suffering and more *fully* in my body and the beautiful world around me.

So, what's your why? Why do you want to create a more wellful life? Take a few moments to think about this. If the idea of living freer and more fully resonates for you, perhaps you might ask why you want to live more freely and fully. What will that freedom and fullness bring to you physically and emotionally? Write your answers and thoughts on a piece of paper and pin it up somewhere that you can see easily every day.

We'll begin our Wellfulness journey outside of ourselves, finding conscious awareness around our food, body and movement, and space, then slowly begin to move our focus inwards, looking to our daily routines and rituals, and finally, arriving at our minds.

Studying Yourself

Each of us is different in physical body, interests of the mind and passions of the heart. Equally, when all of these are in harmony on an individual level, we can create the perfect foundation from which to achieve ultimate holistic wellness. When you step back and consider each of these elements together, you gain a more holistic view of how the things you do – what you eat, how you exercise, and so on – fit into your life. If you can identify the things that serve and nourish you in your body, your mind and your heart, you can empower yourself to fill your life with healthy habits and rituals that not only work for you physically, but that you also find enjoyable, interesting and meaningful. And when you fill your life with activities and things that tick all of these boxes, then they have a much better chance of becoming a natural, long-standing part of your life.

Together, we are going to move through each area of your life to give you a unique blueprint from which to create a holistic wellness plan that works authentically for you on every level. And the understanding and knowledge you gain will come from within.

At the end of the previous chapter, I mentioned the modern habit of constantly seeking knowledge from outside of ourselves, especially when it comes to health and wellness. But while there is, of course, space for procuring information and learning from others, wisdom cannot be found in this way. For example, when you sense danger, when you eat bad food, or when you love something or someone deeply, you don't need anyone to tell you it is so – you just know.

In Eastern philosophy, the study of the 'self' is often as important as eating, keeping clean or exercising. Wisdom is something that is, and always has been, within and it is also something we can practise building a stronger connection to. This is why so many of us keep coming back to ancient Eastern practices, such as yoga and Buddhist meditation. They provide us with the very important tool of mindful awareness, which can create a conversation between the body, mind and our inner wisdom. And modern science confirms this. Research has proven that the techniques of mindfulness can help us understand and get to know ourselves on a deeper level.

PRACTISING ENLIGHTENMENT

There are eight limbs of yoga in total, and the physical practice of yoga (asana) makes up just one of these eight limbs. Alongside the physical asana, the other seven limbs serve to help us find the ultimate goal of yoga – Samadhi, or bliss. I believe that this will mean different things to different people, but a great way to describe it might be to say 'a life without emotional, mental or physical suffering'. My teacher describes it simply as truly being in the present moment. And one important strand from yogic philosophy which we also find in mindfulness, is the idea of 'Svadhyaya', translated to English from Sanskrit as 'self-study'. The practice of studying ourselves and looking within to observe our thoughts and how we feel, is part of the yogic teachings outlined in the 'Niyamas'; a list of positive duties or observances which make up the second limb of yoga. The idea of enlightenment might seem like something only monks in red robes can achieve, but to enlighten simply means to 'put light' on something. 'Svadhyaya', or self-study – essentially, reading this book and trying the practices in it – is enlightenment, by shining a spotlight on who we are, how we think, our habitual patterns and the way we live our lives.

And why would you want to do this? Well, it has been my experience that by bringing conscious awareness to each area of my life, I have empowered myself in the way I live, letting go of what does not serve me and cultivating more of what works for me and nourishes me. I have created a blueprint that is authentic to my body's needs, my mind's needs and my heart's needs, and my health – physical, mental and spiritual – has strengthened and is better aligned. I am living a more conscious life. I have achieved health and life goals that I have only ever dreamed of before. I am living a life that is designed for me, by me. You can do the same.

In a world of increasing pressure and stress, when so often we push ourselves mentally to meet deadlines or targets, it's not unusual to ignore the body – becoming 'deaf' to the messages our physical form is sending us. Why do we sit, hunched over our desks for hours, until we feel stiff? This is a great example of a way that we ignore the body's signals, which are telling us we need to get up and walk around. Even when writing this book, I've found myself doing this, holding on until I was uncomfortable, trying to get a few more paragraphs written. How did this serve me? I could write the paragraphs, probably quicker and better with a clearer head, when I returned from the walk my body was telling me I needed, rather than waiting until I was really uncomfortable.

Equally, we ignore our minds, too. We go along with social plans that we find tedious and buy products we've been told we need, but know we'll never actually use. Or worse still, we move through life on autopilot, never really thinking on any level about what we do or why, from the places we visit and food we eat to the people we spend time with.

A Wellness Practice

LEARNING TO LISTEN: A MEDITATION

The trick of meditation isn't to empty the mind, but to practise focusing the mind through concentration. This is a beautifully simple way to learn how to meditate, through listening to the sounds around you. It also begins to train the mind to listen with inquisitiveness, a tool we'll be using in a big way in your Wellfulness project.

one

Set a timer for 2 minutes. Find a comfortable position on the floor or sit on a chair and close your eyes. Now bring your attention to the sounds around you. Don't strain to hear, just allow the sounds to come to you. What do you hear?

two

Your mind might wander, but that's completely normal. If you find yourself drifting or lost in a thought, smile and come back to listening to the sounds without judging yourself. You can do this as many times as you need to – it's all a part of mindfulness.

three

Once the 2 minutes are up, spend a few moments writing down answers to the following questions:

- ☐ What did you hear?
- ☐ Were the sounds constant or changing?
- ☐ Which sounds did you like? How did you react to them?
- ☐ Which sounds did you dislike? How did you deal with them?

- ☐ Did you feel neutral to any of the sounds? Note down which and perhaps describe what they felt like to you.

four

Now set your timer for another 2 minutes.

Close your eyes once more and bring your attention to the sounds again, this time noticing if you can listen without judgement or bias towards the sounds you hear.

Can you lean into the sounds you dislike and not try to push them away? Can you just allow whatever you hear to be there without liking or disliking it, but simply being interested in and curious about it?

When you've finished, again explore your experience by noting down your feelings and reactions. Ask yourself:

- ☐ What was that like?
- ☐ How did it feel to practise acceptance around both pleasant and unpleasant sounds?
- ☐ What did you discover when you applied curiosity to your feelings?

Take back control

When I was younger I'd go horse riding at the weekends. For a few months, I took out a young horse called River, a cheeky four-year-old Appaloosa – brown and white with a beautiful spotted pattern. He was mischievous, not very good at taking orders and scared of his own shadow. I'd often come home with scratches and bruises, after he'd trampled through holly bushes and narrow gates to avoid his biggest fear in life – puddles – and he'd regularly throw me off when he didn't feel like trotting. I tried for weeks to build his confidence, until one afternoon I ended up in hospital after he'd bucked me off, headfirst onto the ground. I lay there, feeling him jump over me, convinced he was going to trample me, followed by the longest seconds of my life, waiting to see if I could move my legs. That was the end of my relationship with River.

Then a few years ago, I read a Zen Buddhist story that reminded me of him. It tells the tale of a horse, galloping down the road with a rider on its back, who looks like he has somewhere important to be. A bystander calls out, 'Where are you going?' to which the man on the horse replies, 'I don't know! Ask the horse.'

I know how that rider felt – there was one boss in my relationship with River, and it wasn't me! But this Zen story is a great analogy for life, too: the horse symbolizes our habits – the things we may do from day to day, without thinking

too deeply about them – the food we eat, the way we get ready for bed, the people we spend time with, the route we take to work and the way we react to situations. We often live at the mercy of our habits, which are embedded and confirmed in our lives, not with our conscious intention but by our environment, society and mindless learned behaviour. The rider's horse (or habit), is taking him to a destination he isn't even aware of! But he is used to this – it is how things have always been, what he's always known. That doesn't mean, however, that it is right for him or that it serves him.

The moral of the story is that you can learn how to take back the reins (your control) and let the horse (your habits) know who's boss. You can understand why you do the things you do, how they make you feel and know whether they serve and nourish you or set you back and even hurt you. Essentially, you're the boss, you've always been the boss, so wake up and take charge!

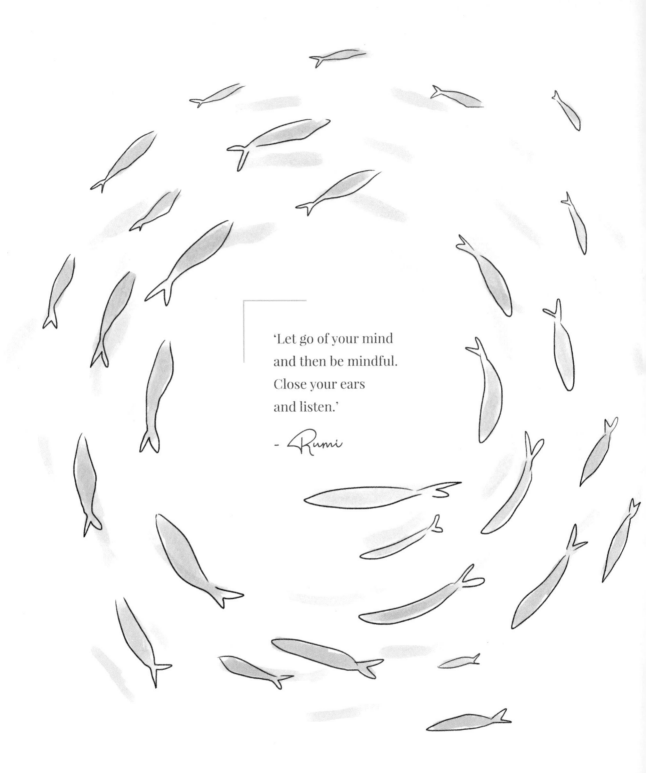

'Let go of your mind
and then be mindful.
Close your ears
and listen.'

- Rumi

Discover what serves YOU

So, what habits are carrying you off to an unknown and undesired destination? We all have mindless habits and behaviours. That's completely normal. And every habit or routine – every meal, every workout and every person we spend time with or place we visit – has an impact on the way we feel. Some will be easy to spot and others will take years to become aware of and unravel. That's what Wellfulness has the power to do – help you become aware of and find freedom from the conditioning and the habits that do not serve you.

So, what's serving you? This is a question you need to ask again and again. When you find the practices that truly work for you, you are able to live a more balanced and authentically healthy life, both physically and mentally.

In the West, as our research and understanding around the connection between body and mind grows, we are increasingly coming to embrace a more holistic approach to wellness, seeing body, mind and spirit as one, in the way that health is viewed by the ancient Eastern practices of yoga, mindfulness, and Ayurvedic and Chinese medicine.

On the following pages is the chart 'How Does Your Practice Feel'. This chart shows how your wellness practices might feel in body, mind and heart. I believe that in order for any practice to follow a holistic path, and have a long-term place in your life, it must tick one or more of the bullet points in at least two of the 'positive' columns (page 40).

On the other hand, a practice that does not serve you, might cause you to feel one or more of the bullet points listed in the 'negative' columns (page 41). With new awareness, you might recognize that you need to make a change in order to negate the points you've resonated with. That change might be to let go of whatever practice, food, exercise, ritual or person this chart is bringing your awareness to. In some instances, you won't be able to let go of negative feelings. But, as you work your way through this book, you will learn about mindful tools, such as conscious acceptance and compassion, which will help you to discover your own unique needs, and how to apply them to a unique wellness plan.

POSITIVE

BODY
physical

- [ ] It feels good in your body

- [ ] It makes a positive impact on your physical health e.g. lowered blood pressure, immune system, clearer skin, visceral fat around your organs, less bloated etc

- [ ] It gives you physical energy

- [ ] It improves your physical capability e.g. flexibility, coordination or strength

- [ ] It makes you feel more comfortable or confident in your body

MIND
mental

- [ ] It interests you

- [ ] It stimulates you mentally

- [ ] It improves your mental/ emotional resilience or confidence

- [ ] It makes you feel less stressed

- [ ] It makes you more productive

- [ ] It makes you feel more patient, open-minded

- [ ] It increases your knowledge or skillset

- [ ] It helps you to deal with and respond, rather than react to difficult situations

HEART
soul & happiness

- [ ] It makes your heart sing

- [ ] It tastes, feels, sounds or looks good to you

- [ ] It gives your spirit or your soul energy

- [ ] It feels authentic to who you are

- [ ] It aligns with your values and what you believe in

- [ ] It adds to your inner wisdom, or helps you grow as a person

- [ ] It makes you feel part of something

- [ ] It makes you more compassionate towards yourself and others

- [ ] It gives you purpose

NEGATIVE

BODY
physical

- ☐ It feels bad in your body

- ☐ It makes a negative impact on your physical health e.g. causes bloating, headaches, unhealthy weight gain or loss, heightened blood pressure or risk of serious disease

- ☐ It tires you energetically

- ☐ It makes you feel less comfortable or confident in your body

MIND
mental

- ☐ It bores you

- ☐ It makes you less emotionally resilient or confident

- ☐ It makes you feel more anxious or stressed

- ☐ It makes you less productive

- ☐ It makes you feel impatient

- ☐ It makes you less open-minded

- ☐ It doesn't encourage or nurture your knowledge or skillset

- ☐ It triggers you to react rather than respond to difficult situations

HEART
soul & happiness

- ☐ It makes you feel a negative emotion; drained, sad, ashamed

- ☐ It tastes, feels, sounds or looks bland or negative

- ☐ It drains your spirit or your soul energy

- ☐ It feels unauthentic to who you are, you don't agree with it or it opposes your values

- ☐ It stops you from growing as a person

- ☐ It makes you feel disconnected from people or the world

- ☐ It makes you selfish or less compassionate

- ☐ It creates a negative inner dialogue and promotes self-hate or low self-worth

Finding Alignment in Body, Heart and Mind

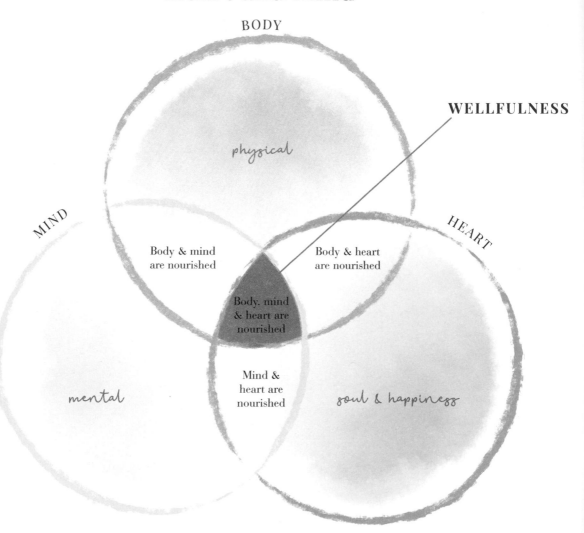

The Wheels of Wellfulness

From working through the columns on the two charts, you should now have a clearer idea of how your body, mind and heart might feel when they're being nourished and served – and when they're not. Feel free to refer back to the charts whenever you need to, as you move through your personal Wellfulness Project, and especially as you begin to use the tool I've created to map out your unique wellness plan – the Wheels of Wellfulness. This interactive tool will help you to look within and observe how the things you do make you feel within your body, mind and heart. By finding a deeper awareness around how your actions make you feel in each of these areas, you will awaken to whether the choices you make and way you live your life are serving you, nourishing you and, ultimately, working for you.

Look at the Wheels of Wellfulness diagram. In the centre, where the three circles intersect, lies the 'beating heart' of Wellfulness. Ideally, this is where you should want to be living your life from – the place where body, mind and heart are aligned. When you find habits and practices that serve you in each of these areas, you find yourself in the centre of the Wheels of Wellfulness – the heart of holistic health.

How to use the Wheels of Wellfulness to figure out if a practice is 'Wellful' and serves you on a holistic level:

Step 1: Ask yourself how the practice or idea makes you feel in body, mind, and heart, and fill in in each relevant circle.

one
How do I feel
in my body?

two
How do I feel
in my mind?

three
How do I feel
in my heart?

Step 2: Decide whether the practice or idea serves you by ticking or crossing the relevant intersections. See my examples on the following pages. If you can tick all three (grey) outer intersections, you can then tick the middle intersection (yellow) and you know your practice serves you holistically in body, mind and heart. If you can only tick one or two of the outer intersections, you then have a chance to choose whether you can improve on or adapt your practice so that it serves you better in the area/s that is lacking for you. If you can't tick any outer intersections, your practice or idea isn't serving, nourishing or working for you on a holistic level. Awareness = empowerment!

BODY

My legs feel sluggish
and I've got shin splints
————————
I'm tired and my lower back hurts
————————
I've got no strength or tone in my upper body
————————
I never run far enough to really improve my fitness

MIND

HEART

I dread my run all day
————————
I'm so bored when I am
running, all I can think
about is when it will be over

Thinking about going for
a run makes my heart sink
————————
I dont have fun when
I'm running
————————
My only joy comes from
when its over

The Wheels of Wellfulness: My Running Practice

Here are my Wheels of Wellfulness examining something that's a key part of my life – exercise. I live in Greenwich in London, the home of the start of the London Marathon. Every year, running fever abounds in the area. With this energy all around me, I became driven to go running. But I'd spend all day dreading my daily run. When it came to lacing up my trainers, my heart would sink. Then I'd spend the whole run thinking a combination of 'Ow, this hurts,' 'God I'm so bored!' and 'When will it end?' I never ran far enough to build up my fitness past a certain level – my mind made sure I stopped before that ever happened – and so my body didn't ever really respond to this kind of movement.

Putting all this into a Wheels of Wellfulness diagram, this is how my running practice looked. Everything I thought and felt about running is negative. This is shown by the three grey crosses in the areas where the body, mind and heart circles intersect, so where the circles all meet in the centre is a big red cross.

BODY

I feel so energised afterwards

———

My body feels great during practice as
I stretch and work my body

———

I'm getting stronger and I can see definition in my body

———

My lower back pain has gone

MIND

HEART

I always look forward to my
class

———

My mind becomes more still
during and after my practice

———

I love learning new poses
and I'm fascinated by the
different postures

Yoga inspires me

———

When I practice on my own I feel
very at peace and content

———

I feel so happy going to class
with my friends and I laugh the
whole way through

The Wheels of Wellfulness: My Yoga Practice

I looked at another physical exercise I practised – yoga – and applied the Wheels of Wellfulness tool to that too. You can see how different it looks now! I've got three grey ticks where I serve all three areas of body, mind and heart, and so my yoga practice sits in the heart of the wheels, shown here with the golden tick.

Running and yoga are both forms of physical exercise, both forms of movement meditation, yet they do different things for different people. When I brought mindful awareness to how they made me feel, it was clear that one was serving me more than the other in every way, and so my health blueprint began to take shape. To feel better in my body, to stay interested enough to keep doing it, and to have fun at the same, I clearly need more yoga and less running. This is a simple conclusion to which, until I had applied the Wheels of Wellfulness, I had been completely blind.

The first steps

Through using our inner wisdom, we become more awake to how we are living, and it's from this place that we can create transformation in our lives. So, think of something you do regularly as part of your wellness regime. It can be anything – a Sunday walk or your everyday breakfast – it doesn't have to be something you think is bad or good. The key is to come at it without judgement or preference and look at it with fresh eyes.

Now apply it to a Wheels of Wellfulness diagram by asking how it makes you feel in body, mind and heart. Once you've written down your feelings about your regular habit or practice, you can figure out whether it is working well for you (or not!). If it isn't working, ask what you need to do. You don't have to make any big decisions or changes immediately, this is just a practice before we move on to exploring Wellfulness in greater detail and creating your unique wellness plan in Part 3 of this book. Here, just come at this exercise with a sense of playful and kind curiosity, as if through a child's eyes. If you find this difficult, that's okay. Try practicing the meditation for tuning into your inner wisdom (see opposite) once a day to become more comfortable with looking within and connecting to your inner guide.

A Wellness Practice

TUNING INTO YOUR INNER WISDOM: A MEDITATION

I like to do this every morning on waking. I actually love to do it in the shower, which is a very mindful practice in itself. If you can, try to do this short meditation, or the 'Learning to listen' meditation (see page 35), or the mirror practice for self-study and mind-body connection (see page 114) daily. Meditation at the same time each day can be helpful in keeping up the practice.

one

Close your eyes and take a deep breath to anchor yourself. Then imagine your mind is a pool of water.

two

Drop a pebble into your pool (of awareness) – small, smooth and grey. The pebble represents a question: 'How am I, right now?'

three

Let this question drop gently into the pool, watch it sink all the way to the bottom – to the edges of your awareness. Allow it to sit there for a moment.

four

Observe the ripples that expand out from the centre of that pebble or question – concentric circles of answering thoughts. Watch each one without preference or bias, observing them get bigger and bigger until they eventually fade. As they disappear at the outer edges of your pool of awareness, let them go.

five

Now drop in another pebble. This one asks 'How do I feel?' Ask it a few times if need be, and allow the question to slowly sink into your awareness.

six

Again, bring your attention to the answering ripples of thought, without judgement or preference. Just notice, and let the answers go.

seven

Simply stay with the feeling. If you find yourself getting caught up in stories attached to the feeling, ask, 'Where does this feeling live in my body?' Stay curious only to the sensations of the feeling, not the stories or 'whys' that surround it. Simply observe, without judgement or needing to change anything.

eight

Inhale, exhale. Feel a sense of loving kindness towards yourself and send yourself a warm hug of compassion if any negative feelings came up for you here. Open your eyes with your newly discovered awareness.

Take it further

What happens when you discover that a practice only serves two out of three elements of your body, mind and heart? For example, let's say that you find running makes your heart sing, feels great in your body and works for your physical fitness, but that it's a bit boring, so you can only tick the intersection between the body and heart circles on your Wheels of Wellfullness diagram. You've empowered yourself through listening to your inner guidance and from here you can ask yourself what you need to do to stop being bored, such as finding an interesting podcast to listen to while you run.

Perhaps you know the boredom makes you resistant to running and so you don't run very often. You may, therefore, feel that in order to be healthy, you need to find another form of exercise that interests you, so that it can be a natural and enjoyable part of your life. Or perhaps the feeling of joy you get when you finish your run and the physical benefits far outweigh the mental boredom. Together, these two elements can still get you out running every day, so some acceptance around finding it a bit boring is what you decide you need.

If no intersecting areas are ticked, because something only serves one area – for example, running works for you on a physical level, but you find it boring and your heart sinks when it's time to put on your trainers – then again ask, 'What do I need?' Do you need to let go of the practice? Or can you adjust it somehow so that it does serve you in another or both of the other areas? My running didn't serve me in body, mind or heart. It was only when I brought my full awareness to this, by using the Wheels of Wellfulness to look deeply at my own experience, and not what I thought I should be experiencing, that I realized running was not working for me. From there I was able to ask, 'What do I need?' After observing the ripples that spread out from the centre of this question, without judgement or bias, simply observing what was there, I made the conscious and empowering choice to compassionately allow myself to let go of my running practice.

Seek the positive

It could be easy to focus only on the negative, but there is also great power in spending time considering what does serve, nourish and work for you. In realizing what makes you feel great, you empower yourself to continue doing it, and also doing it more often. For example, you might decide that you want to spend more time with someone whose company you enjoy, or to visit a place that inspires new ideas or makes you feel at home, or do a workout that serves your body, heart and mind, or take longer over a specific part of your bedtime routine that makes your heart sing. Don't be afraid to place some awareness on finding an equilibrium between the parts of your life you need to let go of and the things you already do and need to keep or create more of. Life is better in balance!

But always remember we are transient beings – fluid and ever moving. One day you might love running and the next day you can't face it. Try not to get caught up in the stories of 'why?', or ponder over the fact that the last time you ran, your heart was singing, your body vibrating with energy and your mind excited – while now your mind is finding any excuse not to go out and run, your legs feel like lead and your heart is sinking further and further, as you get closer to walking out of that door. You are allowed to change your mind. You don't have to be any fixed 'type' of person. So often we want to put ourselves in boxes and tell ourselves, for example, 'I must run because I like to run,' meanwhile ignoring the fact that you, the real you in this moment (and the only real you there ever is) would rather do something else. Allow yourself to be you, with kindness and without judgement.

Open your eyes

As you begin to bring more awareness to your life, the neural pathways that help you to be more mindful strengthen and, even if you only begin by looking at your health, by thinking about the way you eat, move or sleep makes you feel, it's inevitable that you will begin to question bigger elements or aspects of how you live and bring mindful awareness to those, too. Perhaps you might find yourself bringing a deeper awareness to your career, or your purpose in life, or to your values and beliefs. And sometimes, this can be tough.

In ancient Eastern philosophies, it's often understood that those who seek more awareness or deeper understanding in their lives, can stumble across feelings of discomfort or pain. A wise yogi once explained this as, 'Dust that lands on the skin is harmless, but if one tiny particle gets into the eye, it's very painful.' Essentially, in order to find clarity in your life, you must open our eyes wide and so may become more sensitive. But this is a positive – this sensitivity gives you a special insight that can act as warning light. And by following this book, you are actively looking for these warning lights to help you understand what is and isn't serving and nourishing you in terms of food, exercise and movement, your surroundings and your routines and habits. But alongside this, you must remember that you will uncover more truth than you would if you kept your eyes closed – and the truth might not always be what you want to find, such as an allergy to your favourite snack, or the realization that a relationship is making you unhappy and needs to change.

STARTING YOUR WELLFULNESS JOURNEY

You have the power to change

In his book *The Heart of Yoga*, the TKV Desikachar writes, 'The person who is not searching for clarity does not even know what brings him or her happiness or sorrow.' We might be at the point now where we have no clarity, where all we know is that we feel unhappy, or uncomfortable in our skin, or tired all the time, or impatient with life, but we don't know why. Equally, we might know we feel happy or content, we might have clear skin or great friendships, but again, never have considered why. When we search for clarity in our lives and bring awareness to the things we do, we empower ourselves to create more of the great stuff, because we understand why it works for us.

Ignorance can be a comfortable place to live from, yet we run the risk of missing out on health and happiness by remaining in the safety of that ignorance. Sometimes your quest for clarity around what makes you feel healthy and happy in body and mind might take courage to pursue. You might discover that you need to change the way you eat in order to feel better in your body, but encounter resistance to that change. Or you might realize you spend most of your time with someone who makes you feel bad about yourself and not enough time with someone who makes you smile, but you find it difficult to contemplate changing those dynamics because you're stuck in a certain social routine. Yet despite having experienced both of these realizations myself, the benefits I've reaped through the changes I've made have far outweighed the discomfort I felt in realizing I needed to change (or accept) them in the first place – or in making those changes happen. I'd have never known those benefits had I not found the courage to change.

So, I want you to know how much compassion I feel for you and the Wellfulness journey ahead of you, and how much I respect your commitment to creating a happier, healthier, freer and fuller life. It makes my heart SING! I see you. I see the changes you will make, because I have made them too – and I continue to make them. I see the courage it takes to step outside of the normal routine, the ordinary and the okay, in order to live a bigger, bolder, braver and more extraordinary life. You have the power to change. You just need to realize that power comes from turning your gaze inwards, by looking deep inside yourself in order to find that guiding light – your inner wisdom.

Part Three
Exploring Wellfulness

'You do not have to walk on
your knees, for a hundred miles
through the desert, repenting.
You only have to let the soft animal
of your body, love what it loves'

- Mary Oliver

CREATING YOUR UNIQUE WELLNESS PLAN

In this section we will create together a master wellness plan, or blueprint for each area of your life: food, body, space, ritual and mind. We will look at each practice, habit, routine or new idea, to see where it sits within the intersections of your Wheels of Wellfulness, so that you begin to get a picture of what works for you, what doesn't, what you need, and what you might want to consciously change. We'll move through each of the main areas in your life together, applying this method as we go, so that by the end of the book you'll have a visual map that acts as your blueprint for a truly unique wellness plan, that's designed, tried and tested specifically for you, by you.

Inhale. Exhale. Let's begin...

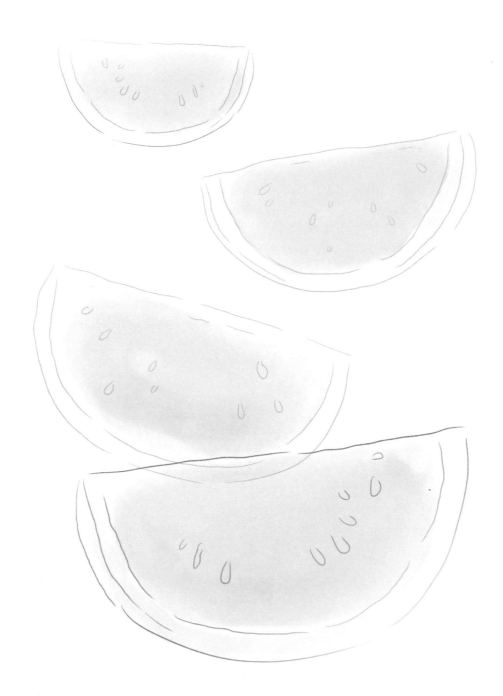

Food

With everything going on in the world, it can be easy to think that there are far more important things than food to worry about. Of course, that can be seen as a valid response to an obsession with 'clean' and 'conscious' eating. There's even an eating disorder called orthorexia, a compulsion with avoiding any food that might be considered unhealthy or harmful. I've even had to resist a tendency to look too closely at what I eat, telling myself, 'What a first-world problem to have!' And yet, I also find myself spending a lot of my day thinking about food, from trying to choose healthy options to pondering which ingredients I need for dinner.

But food should have an important place in your life. Aside from being a source of comfort and joy, food is essential for each and every one of us. We all must eat. Food is a source of life, fuelling us with energy and playing a massive role in how our bodies and minds perform. So, how does the food you eat make you feel?

Diets don't work

When I was in my early twenties and wanted to lose weight, the answer was 'eat meat!' It was meat for breakfast, meat for lunch and meat for dinner. So I decided to try a high-protein diet of mainly meat and the odd egg or a little tuna for a change. The only carbohydrates allowed were in a small bowl of gruel-like oatmeal for breakfast, with vegetables being gradually re-introduced weeks later. I lost weight and I lost it quickly – in fact, it's the only time I've ever really seen results from dieting. From the outside, my body looked great. On the inside, however, it felt awful. There's nothing like the sensation of filling a heavy, sluggish stomach, which feels like it's been trying to digest old leather for weeks on end, with yet more meat. But hey, why did that matter? I'd lost weight!

It was impossible to keep up my diet in the long term and that's one of the main issues with diets. So many of them, especially the ones that leave out major food groups or ask you to eat just one kind of food repeatedly, aren't sustainable. Why? The answer is that they don't serve the mind, body or heart. Your mind gets bored and tells stories of deprivation or deserving, leading you to temptation and treats. As meals become less interesting, eating becomes soulless and you lose the passion to continue in your heart. And your body starts to feel sluggish and can even crave the things you're missing. If you're dieting, maybe you should try using the Wheels of Wellfulness (see page 42) to explore how it is serving you now. Remember – be curious and kind to yourself.

During my high-animal-protein diet, my body had been sending me signals for weeks on end that I hadn't noticed, or had chosen not to listen to. Firstly, I broke out in spots and my skin started to lose its glow and look lifeless. I had little energy and found it difficult to exercise. I found myself craving vegetables and fruit. Then I noticed my hair started to thin and become brittle (research has found that a low-carb diet can cause hair loss through nutritional deficiencies). I could feel my attention drifting at work and I remember sitting almost zombie-like on a bench, staring into space, while I ate my lunch. Any joy I had for eating had disappeared. There was no passion there, no love. It was as if my life was becoming duller with each meal.

It took a couple of months for me to take notice of what my body was telling me. This diet had slowly been removing my zest for life – making me feel awful on the inside and even changing who I was as a person. I was becoming passionless, drained and often grumpy. It ended with a holiday, on which a very tempting bread basket broke me on the third morning. Should the food we eat really be a source for daily mental struggle? For so many of us it is, but wouldn't it be so liberating if it wasn't?

A few years and a little mindful awareness later, I became first a vegetarian and then moved on to a plant-based diet. I now literally have nightmares about eating meat, which is not altogether surprising after my diet experience, but it highlights just how wrong it was for me. That's not to say it wouldn't be right for someone else. Depending on body type, goals, enjoyment and whether you eat meat and animal products or not, a high-protein, low-carb day-to-day menu might be exactly what works for your body, mind and heart. We are unique creatures.

I now look back at that diet and see it as a wonderful lesson. It was a real kick-start on my journey towards a more mindful life. Food was the first place where I began to have a conversation with my body, mind and heart. It was a place from which to start asking, 'Is this serving me?'

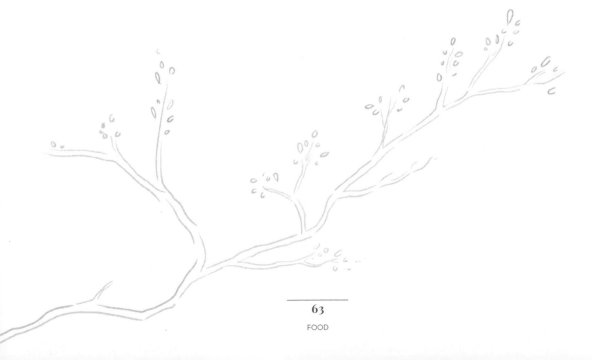

Mindful eating

Food is a great place to begin to practise mindful awareness – mostly because it's enjoyable and there are so many elements to it – smell, taste, texture and even the sound of it as it moves around a plate. You may have heard of mindful eating. It's a wonderful practice and very simple to do, spending a meal bringing all your awareness to your food – something we very rarely do. In a restaurant or at home, you'll probably talk and listen to music while eating, which can move your focus away from the food. The taste of the food may meander into your awareness, but the sensation of it will be dampened by your attention being taken elsewhere. But when you eat mindfully, you will often find that the taste of the food is heightened as you bring your full awareness to it.

I lead retreats on which I will drop a group into a period of silence that extends over an early morning walk and into breakfast. At first it feels awkward as the group struggles with wanting to fill the silence with small talk, but as this subsides I always sense the point where everyone begins to relax. At breakfast, I can see them really enjoying their food, their full attention on it, interacting with it – consciously considering additions of cinnamon, syrup or fruit to their porridge. It's a joy to watch and we often have the most fascinating conversations afterwards about how tastes had exploded in their mouths, or how they had never noticed before that they like cinnamon so much. Very often they try something new, because they are curious, and discover that they love it.

Mindful eating is a wonderful way to practise mindfulness and begin to build the neural pathways that support a more focused awareness of your present experience. But there is one limitation to mindful eating. You may be aware of the food, of how it tastes, smells and feels, and perhaps of how satisfying that food is, but you are not prompted to take that present awareness within yourself to a deeper level. The real magic of mindful eating happens when you begin to place your awareness on how food makes you feel.

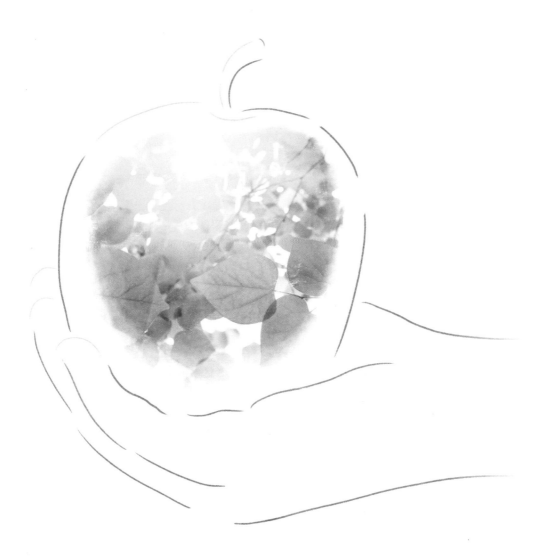

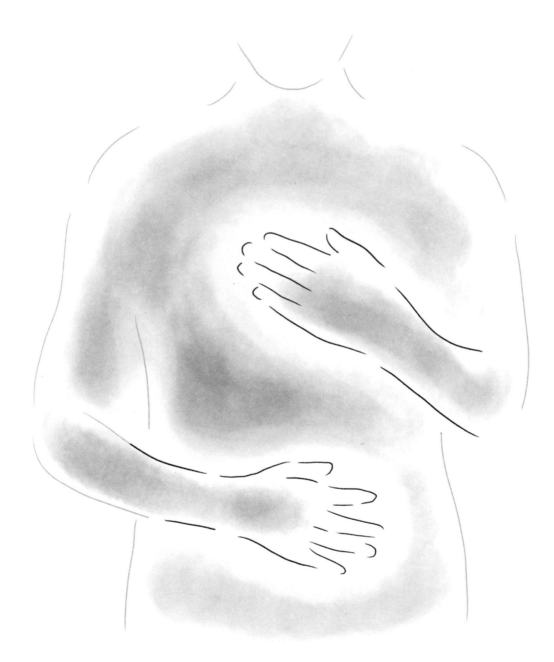

EXPLORING WELLFULNESS

Intuitive eating

You may have heard of intuitive eating. It is about using your intuition – trusting your inner wisdom – to make choices about food based on how it feels in your body, without judgement and without influence from any diet culture. Becoming more mindful is an important tool when it comes to intuitive eating, in that you cannot hear your body's inner wisdom if you are not tuned into the present moment. Once you are, you can begin to listen to the information your body is giving you. This is called interoception and, for many of us, it isn't something we're deeply tuned into. But by using Wellfulness, you can begin to listen more closely to your body and the signals it sends you about how your food makes you feel.

Intuitive eating is the difference between listening and being a slave to what our mind wants (sugar, cake, chips!) and what our body wants (fruit! water! fibre!). By learning to listen to these 'interoceptive' messages and signals from our body during and after eating, we are able to begin to hear important messages about what our body needs, what foods do and do not work for us, and even information on how and where we eat.

So, intuitive eating takes mindful eating a step further, from being in the present moment and using the practice of eating as a tool to develop our mindful muscle, to applying the skill of mindfulness to help us pay attention to how the food we eat and the way we eat it makes our body feel, in order to guide ourselves towards eating for our body's needs rather than our mind's wants.

An interactive meditation with a difference! With your next meal, why not give yourself the gift of a mindful eating experience. Draw or print out the Wheels of Wellfulness (see page 42) on a piece of paper and make the circles big enough to write in, keeping a pen near you.

one

Switch off your phone, tablet or computer and any music, so there is no screen or sound to distract you. Sit comfortably with just your food.

two

Before digging in, look at the food in front of you with curiosity. Try to imagine you are a looking at this meal as a baby or toddler might, as someone who hasn't tried what they're about to eat before. What does the food look like? Smell like? Take a moment to notice. Now ask, 'How does this make me feel?' Think about this question in terms of each area of the Wheels of Wellfulness – body, mind and heart (see page 42). Write down how the food makes you feel in each of the main circles, leaving the areas where the circles intersect for now.

three

Start eating. What are you drawn to first? Maybe you want to pick up some food first with your fingers, to feel it or experience it in a different way. Maybe you don't want to do that. However you feel is okay! Just write down your thoughts, feelings and any sensations in the circles of your Wheels of Wellfulness. Chew mindfully, with playful interest. Keep your attention on the tastes, sounds, smells, textures and sight of your food with an unbiased curiosity and continue to ask yourself, throughout the meal, 'How do I feel?' in your body, mind and heart.

four

Your feelings might change as you eat. That's normal! Allow yourself to be fluid – your only job is to notice these changes, with compassion and without judgement.

five

At the end of your meal, ask yourself one last time, 'How do I feel?' and add any last comments to each circle.

BODY

I didn't realize how
hungry I was!

———————

All these veggies are filling me up but
I don't feel sluggish – I actually feel
quite energized

———————

I feel a bit bloated at the end

MIND

HEART

I've never tried
Buddha bowl before.
It's fun!

———————

I really love all the different
colours and flavours

———————

The aubergine is my
favourite bit

———————

I'm eating really quickly

Hello soul food!
This makes me feel
so comforted

———————

It feels good in my heart to
make a healthy choice

———————

I know I'm doing something good
for the world by eating veggie
one day a week – and living
by my values makes
me feel great!

The Wheels of Wellfulness: my mindful eating meditation

Step 1: The first step is to ask yourself how your meal makes you feel in your body, mind and soul.

Opposite is an example of the Wheels of Wellfulness I completed while eating a veggie Buddha bowl. Now take a look at your Wheels of Wellfulness and, taking all your notes into account, ask yourself, 'Did this meal serve me? Did it nourish my body? Did it nourish my mind? Did it nourish my soul?'

Step 2: Work out whether you are being served on a holistic level; which intersections can you tick?

Does your experience sit in one of the outer intersections or in the holistic heart in the middle, where body, mind and heart are all nourished? Maybe it doesn't sit in any of the intersections? Wherever you find yourself is fine. Be curious, be interested and be compassionate. If you need some help, refer back to pages 42–3 for how the Wheels of Wellfulness work.

In my example here, you can see that eating my Buddha bowl serves me in body, mind and heart, so I've gone ahead and ticked all the intersections on my Wheels of Wellfulness; mind and body, body and heart, heart and mind. As they are all served, I can then tick the middle golden inner intersection – this meal completely serves me fully and holistically!

Tuning into interoception

Your body sends signals and messages to your mind all the time, whether you're awake or asleep. It is constantly communicating with you, telling you what it needs. Interoception is the word used to describe the information sent by our body and your perception of that information, which in turn leads to how you feel, whether that's hungry, thirsty, tired or threatened in some way. Yet we often fail to notice what our bodies are telling us. I will reach for a packet of biscuits, when what I actually need is a glass of water – only to find myself waking up from thirst in the middle of the night.

In more severe cases we can, for example, misread the body telling us that it is tired, pushing on with a job, without allowing ourselves to rest. This overworking can lead to negative emotions in the mind, which might then be misinterpreted as feelings of depression, when all we really need is to rest and get some sleep. This disconnection between body and mind has been studied in depth and weak interoception is common in mental health disorders. It has also been shown that those with greater ability to interpret interoceptive messages from the body have more potential to respond to those messages in appropriate ways that lead to better mental health.

You might habitually and mindlessly eat foods because they taste nice yet make your body feel sluggish, simply because you always have, and have never stopped to weigh up which one you are happy to compromise on. You might, like me, reach for a snack when actually you're just thirsty, or deprive yourself of food on a diet when your body is calling out for nourishment. It's as if you're not quite tuned into the same frequency that your body is broadcasting on. You get the odd fuzzy message now and then, but the subtler messages are lost in transmission.

One zen student said,
'My teacher is the best.
He can go days without eating.'

The second said,
'My teacher has so much
self-control, he can go days without sleep.'

The third said,
'My teacher is so wise that he eats when
he's hungry and sleeps when he's tired.'

- Zen story

It will often take a bigger signal, or a call for help, from your body to get your attention. After finding one too many flecks of grey in my hair, I started taking a copper supplement, having heard that it was great for preserving natural hair colour. I took my first tablet, then felt a slight pang of sickness. But it passed and I didn't think about it again. The next day I took another tablet. I immediately felt sick again and, this time, my body truly let me know about it. I then remembered having felt sick before. It was as if my body had tried to tell me once and I hadn't quite got the message, so the second time around my body made sure I noticed and understood what it was telling me. I thanked it that day and marvelled at its inner wisdom, feeling compassion for how it takes care of itself and vowing to listen more closely in the future.

But the signals your body sends you aren't always that obvious. At work, I regularly ate an apple after lunch. I'd look forward to it all morning. Then, every evening, I'd drive home and, without fail, have to loosen my clothes and my seatbelt, as my stomach was so bloated and painful. I didn't get it. I ate healthily, I exercised. So why did my belly get so bloated? Going to bed every night, having visually put on about two stone, started to really get me down. But I couldn't figure out why my bloating was happening. This went on for years, without my even realizing that perhaps my body was trying to tell me something, until it got so painful that my body demanded my attention with stabbing stomach cramps every night.

I realized I had to do something and, after a little research, I discovered that fruit is digested fairly quickly, releasing gases into your gut. So when it is eaten after a meal, these gases can become trapped by other food that takes longer to digest. It is the trapped gases that then cause discomfort and bloating. My body had sent me signals that my lunchtime apple was not serving me, but it was only when I gained the knowledge about how fast fruit is digested that I was empowered to change my habit.

However, the real problem was that I hadn't really listened to my body's inner wisdom. Only as I became more mindful and began to tune into my body, my mind and my heart in a deeper way, was I able to tune into the subtle messages that I had missed for years. Every time I ate an apple, my mouth had itched, my stomach had churned and the bloating had appeared until, finally, I understood what was happening and began to realize that I was slightly intolerant to apples. After so many small adjustments, I learned through listening to the wisdom of my body that the food we fuel our bodies with has a huge impact on how we feel. I don't know about you, but I want to feel great, so it's important that I know which foods work for me and support me.

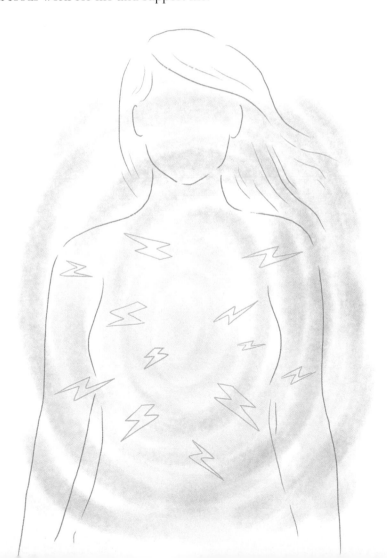

A Wellness Practice
FOOD DIARY: AN ACTIVITY

Want to speak fluent 'you'? Keeping a food diary alongside practising the mindful eating meditation (see page 68) daily, could uncover some fascinating discoveries. To create a truly unique wellness plan when it comes to nutrition and diet, you need to gather your inner wisdom in order to put together a really comprehensive idea of what is and isn't serving you when it comes to the food you eat. This will enable you to create your blueprint for a healthy food plan.

You can do this with your current diet, or you could apply it to any new way of eating you are trying to adopt – like eating less meat – in order to see if it would work for you physically and if it would serve and align with your heart and mind, so that you'll have an idea if you can keep it up in the long term.

one

Over the week or longer, keep a diary of everything you eat and how it makes you feel. Then explore the information you gather by following the mindful eating meditation (see page 68). The longer you keep your diary, the more internal wisdom from your body, mind and heart you'll gather and you'll have a physical 'map' of what food does and what food doesn't serve you, which you may be able to see patterns emerging from.

More importantly, you will also begin to strengthen your mindful muscle, creating new neural pathways and becoming more skilled at being in the present moment, while building that conversation of interoception between body and mind.

two

Fill in your Wheels of Wellfulness after each meal, where possible – how does it make you feel in your body, mind and heart? In no time at all, you won't necessarily need to complete a Wheels of Wellfulness diagram to examine your feelings, but you'll inherently be listening to the inner wisdom and the messages your body is sending you when it comes to food and how it makes your body feel.

three

Now decide whether it serves you in each area, and mark where this meal sits within your Wheel of Wellfulness intersections. Just notice it without judgement or attaching any reasons or stories to it, simply noticing it for a moment. How do you feel?

four

At the end of the day or week, take a look back over your food diary. Notice how you feel in your body. If you are trying a new plan, you could do another final Wheel of Wellfulness that encompasses the whole day or week and how you feel in your body, mind and heart.

five

Now, considering all of this gathered wisdom, ask yourself:

☐ What do I need to consciously accept?

six

☐ Then ask: Where can I send myself some compassion?

seven

☐ And finally: What do I want to consciously change?

eight

☐ How was that? What did you realize?

Eating authentically

The single biggest change in my life, which has transformed my health and had a huge effect on my happiness and confidence, is the moment I realized that I wasn't making authentic decisions when it came to food choices. Essentially, I wasn't being true to myself when it came to what I ate. As I mentioned at the beginning of the chapter, in the past I've forced myself to eat a high-protein diet, which ended in my body sending me strong signals to stop. As I came back to my normal diet, meat still played a large part in my meals, only now I was more aware of how food could make me feel.

Over the next few years, as my mindfulness practice grew and I became more in tune with my body, listening to what it craved, I would choose vegetarian meals more and more. But the real epiphany came when I started to bring awareness to how my mind and my heart felt about the food I was eating. I noticed that a large part of why I cooked meat at home was just habit. It was what most people did. But was I that interested in meat? Not really, and I've heard many people say the same since.

Then I watched a documentary, highlighting some truths about industrial farming that I had never considered. I couldn't watch until the end; the images were that upsetting. But it prompted me to go away and do my own research on where our food comes from and how industrial farming works. As I learned more, I realized that I had been ignorant about how our food is produced and quickly understood that I didn't agree with a lot of the processes involved – the huge quantity of hormones and antibiotics used in rearing livestock; the food livestock ate; the way animals are treated and killed; the psychological effect on humans who are part of that process; and the massive cost of it all to our environment.

In short, the way I was eating did not align with the way I felt or with my values, and that sat uneasily with me. The animal products I was eating did not serve my body, mind or heart when it came to my physical and mental health. When I realized this, I asked myself, 'What do I need to do now?'

The first thing was accepting that I had eaten the wrong food for me for so long. I had been ignorant of where my food came from, perhaps even ignoring the facts about food that tasted so good But now I was aware, there was no ignoring the facts. I had to practise acceptance of the truth and live according to my real values. I had to change things that I liked doing. I took that slowly, but acceptance can be tough. I remember the weekend after I watched that documentary. It was my birthday and I had a trip booked to Italy. It slowly dawned on me that I truly was stuck between a rock and a hard place, wanting to eat the yummy ice cream, cheesy ravioli and pancetta pizzas, yet deep down feeling I couldn't, because I didn't want to go against what I believed in – against who I was. Ultimately, if I was to continue living in a way that went against my inherent belief system, then who was I?

But that didn't stop me from wanting to eat certain things. I was going through a huge transformation, but the world kept turning and the ice cream kept calling. It felt unfair. I had to practise acceptance again and again. The only thing I could do was check in with my mind, body and heart, asking what I needed, then being kind to myself, soothing myself and accepting my situation with compassion. Over time, this acceptance made a home in my heart and I moved on from feeling it was unfair that I couldn't have ice cream or a bacon sandwich. I now eat a healthy, environmentally friendly, plant-based diet, not because I have to but because I want to.

Making the decision to live by my values, even when it meant giving up things that I loved, has been the most life-changing shift I've made during my Wellfulness journey. I'm happier and healthier, both on the inside and outside. From this change, a confidence has been born that I've never experienced before. To live according to your true values is to live authentically and to live authentically is to know yourself deeply.

Your values might be different to mine. There are many ways to eat and many belief systems that align with them. It doesn't really matter what they are, it just matters that you know what they are. From there, you can decide whether or not to live by them, or maybe even realize that you are already, and bring your awareness to how that feels for you.

Conscious compassionate acceptance

When you make something your choice, you decide to change a habit because you want to make that change, not because you have to. When you realize this, you are living your life with conscious, mindful empowerment. But making a change in your diet can allow you to slip into a deprivation mindset. So, alongside the changes I've made, I continuously practise mindful awareness, saying, 'I don't want it' rather than 'I can't have it.'

You can also apply the same process of thinking to things such as food allergies or intolerances, avoiding them because you don't want to be physically ill. But when something is out of bounds completely, because it makes you unwell, this is where practising conscious compassionate acceptance comes in. Acceptance can be a difficult, but in mindfulness, you don't ask yourself to just get over something. In fact, a common mistake when it comes to trying to accept difficult things in life is to push them away, or distract yourself from them with something else.

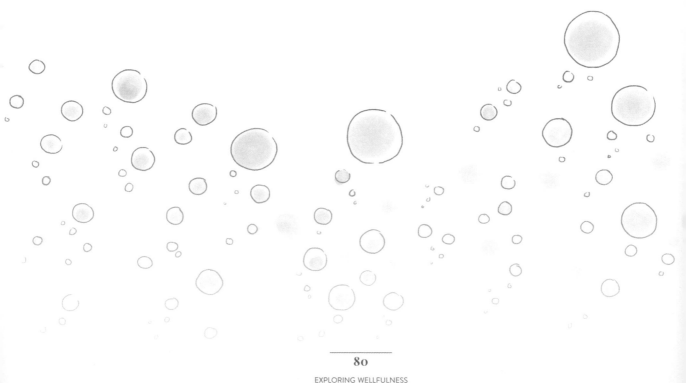

Have you noticed what happens when you push a negative thought or difficult situation away? It usually doesn't go far and often turns on its heel and comes back at you, more forcibly than before. What you resist, tends to persist. In mindfulness, to consciously accept, simply bring your awareness to the hard things in life and sit with them, without feeling that you need to change them, fix them or make them go away. Just by being with them, you learn a superpower that can ease any discomfort you might feel and help it to fade away altogether. That superpower is kindness. When we practise compassion towards ourselves through non-judgement and feel a sense of kindness towards ourselves, we are able to accept situations as they are and find inner peace.

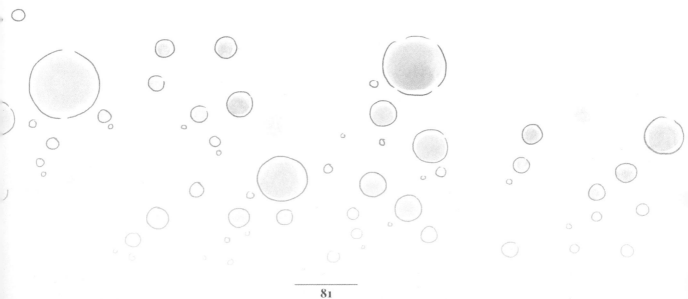

A Wellness Practice
JUNK FOOD ACCEPTANCE: AN ACTIVITY

If you're interested in health and wellness, you probably know that eating a diet crammed with highly processed food is not good for you. It isn't easy to stay away from junk food, but if you want to find greater holistic health, there is usually a point where you realize you need to accept that you can't eat as much of it as you might want to. A little here and there isn't going to harm you, but you need to find a way of being aware not to overdo it, so try using this practice to bring conscious compassionate acceptance to avoiding food that does not serve you.

one

Draw or print out a Wheels of Wellfulness diagram, then sit with it and think about when you indulge in a lot of junk food. Write in the wheels on your diagram how this makes you feel in your body, mind and heart when you eat a lot of it.

two

Now work out if junk food serves you in each area and find out where it sits within the intersections of the circles on your Wheels of Wellfulness for body, mind and heart. Just notice and sit with what you discover for a moment, without trying to come up with any ideas about fixing or judging yourself.

three

☐ Ask yourself, 'How do I feel? What do I need to consciously accept?'

four

☐ Then ask, 'Where can I send myself some compassion here?'

five

☐ And finally ask, 'What do I want to consciously change?'

If you are suffering with, or have suffered with eating disorders in the past, you may prefer to skip this practice and simply bring a sense of gentle and compassionate awareness to each meal you eat, focusing on sending wishes of compassion and kindness to yourself and approaching each sensation you discover with non-judgement and curiosity.

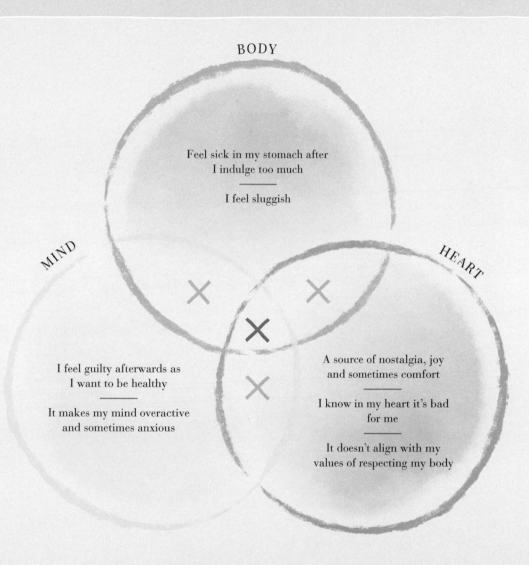

BODY

MIND

HEART

Feel sick in my stomach after
I indulge too much
————
I feel sluggish

I feel guilty afterwards as
I want to be healthy
————
It makes my mind overactive
and sometimes anxious

A source of nostalgia, joy
and sometimes comfort
————
I know in my heart it's bad
for me
————
It doesn't align with my
values of respecting my body

The Wheels of Wellfulness: my junkfood acceptance practice

Food Closing Ritual

Once you've read this chapter and have spent some time thinking and feeling it out in your own life, sit down somewhere comfortable, perhaps with a nice view. This closing ritual will help you to realize where you want to make conscious changes with food and diet. At the end, you'll have a complete and unique Wellfulness Plan for your relationship with food. So, settle down to allow everything you've worked through in this chapter to pour out of your mind and into your journal, or a Wheels of Wellfulness template.

one

Begin by taking a small breathing-space meditation. Close your eyes and inhale deeply to the count of 4, then hold your breath to the count of 4, then exhale to the count of four. Pause briefly and repeat for 3–5 breath cycles. Open your eyes.

two

Now think about your diet; the food you eat, when you eat, how you eat and your values when it comes to food. How does your current diet, or elements of it, make you feel in your body, your mind and your heart? Be conscious to just stay with your feelings, rather than the stories attached to them, and observe without judgement. You can refer back to any Wheels of Wellfulness diagrams you have used while working through this chapter, if you like.

three

Now consider how certain foods, or each approach you have to food, or way you eat, make you feel, in body, mind and heart? Ask: how does it serve me? How does it nourish me? For example, a colourful salad, or making overnight oats for breakfast instead of a sugary bagel on the way to work. Breathe in a sense of wonder and find the joy here! Be curious and playful. Enter each one into the relevant circles, or intersections if they overlap by serving two, or even all three areas of body, mind and heart for you (see an example on page 87).

four

Now ask: 'What's not serving me?' For example, snacking before dinner, or a food that upsets your stomach. What doesn't nourish or serve your body, mind and heart? Place these outside your Wheels of Wellfulness, as I have in the example. Try not to judge these as 'negative', or find ways to change them. Just notice that they exist, and bring those that aren't serving you to mind with a sense of kindness and compassion.

five

Now look at the contents of each circle for body, mind and heart. Everything in the middle intersection where all three wheels overlap, are the things that serve you fully on a holistic level. Everything outside your wheels are the things that do not serve you. The things that sit within one wheel are only serving you on a very basic level, and it's your choice as to whether you continue or adapt them to suit you on a more holistic level. The things outside your wheels do not serve you, and with this new awareness, you can decide whether to accept them, let them go, or adapt them to meet your needs.

CONNECTING WITH FEELINGS

Think about my example of becoming a vegetarian. First, I had to accept, without judgement, that this was where I was. I practised compassion towards myself to help me accept the choices I had made in the past, and the conscious choices I now wanted to make. I then asked myself, 'What do I need now?' I realized that I needed to feel at peace with the food I ate, which meant I needed to live more authentically. It was easy to see the conscious changes I wanted to make from there. I made a change to live by my values when it came to food, which in turn made eating and living authentically possible for me. With this came a sense of real contentment in the way I lived my life. For a friend, her realization during this part of her Wellfulness journey, was seeing that her habit of a daily can of soft drink at her desk made her feel bloated, wired and guilty, as she made the effort to eat less sugar in every other area of her life. She knew this habit wasn't serving her in her body physically, her mind logically or her heart because it didn't align with her feelings about staying healthy and valuing her body. After doing the Wheels of Wellfulness tool together she said, 'Why do I keep doing it? Enough, now that's enough.' She had stepped back out of her habit and seen it with full perspective. Knowledge doesn't create change, feeling creates change. Really try to connect to the feeling when you realize something isn't serving you, and allow that to lead you, rather than your logical mind.

six

It's time to consider the next steps you'll take through conscious acceptance and conscious change. Ask yourself, or journal your answers to the questions below:

☐ Is there anything you need to practice compassionate acceptance around your discoveries? For example, the fact that you realize although you've run most days for five years, it's actually bad for your lower back. Or that until now, you've had a very negative body image.

☐ Now, looking at your wheels, what will you consciously change? For example, you're going try to swim one day a week as it makes you feel relaxed and you love the variety of strokes.

☐ If you feel any resistance to the idea of accepting or changing, simply observe these thoughts and bring back a sense of conscious compassionate acceptance. Can you allow yourself to just observe this resistance and allow it to exist? What's that like?

seven

Think how you will continue to cultivate conscious choice, allowing you to respond, rather than react and act habitually when it comes to food and eating habits, so that when stress, emotion or temptation hit, you can continue to make mindful choices. Perhaps choose to do one of the practices in this chapter on a daily or weekly basis, to strengthen the mindful muscle, which will help you to make food choices that serve and nourish your body, mind and heart. This completed Wheel of Wellfulness is your Food Wellness Plan. Keep it safe – you'll be using it to complete an all-encompassing unique-to-you 'Wellfulness Plan' at the end of the book.

What doesn't serve me?

BODY

Fruit after meals causing bloating

———

Too much junk food

———

Alcohol

———

Dairy: irritates my gut, doesn't align with my values

MIND

recipes that are hard to follow

HEART

Meat

———

Comforting or treating myself with food: I deserve more than that

———

Palm oil - it doesn't align with my values

BODY

High-protein foods
——
High-fat foods
——
All the vegetables

MIND

HEART

Eating mindfully
——
Home cooked, fresh
ingredients
——
Vegetables & lots of colour
on my plate
——
Healthy homemade snacks
——
Plant-based meals

Trying new recipes
——
Interesting snacks
——
New research

Sustainably
packaged foods
——
International
cuisine

Junk food in small
amounts
——
Socializing with
friends

Wheels of Wellfulness: my unique Wellfulness plan for my food

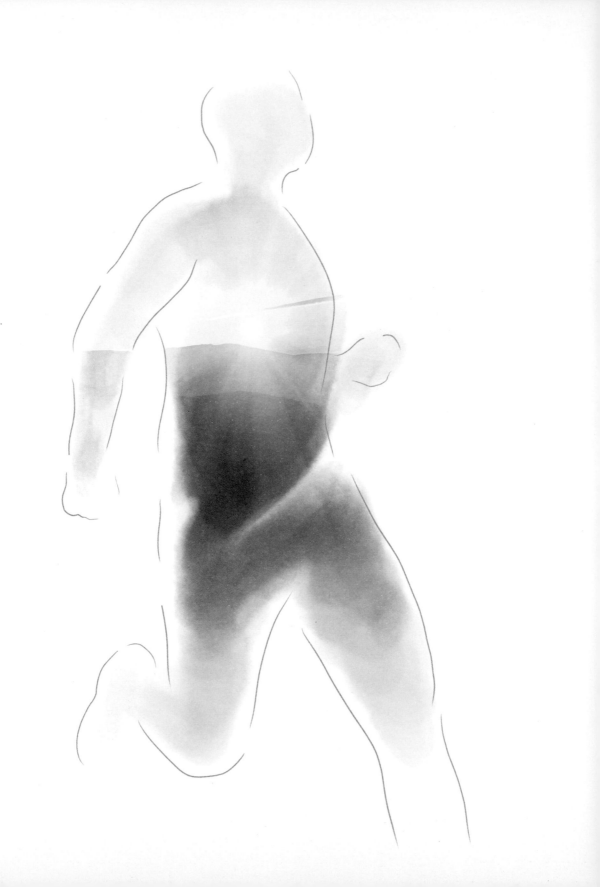

Body

Over the course of a week, we might sit for hours on end at work, in more or less one position, then once away from our desks, we push our bodies physically, carrying heavy bags or at the gym – making them work harder and faster to look or feel better. But we rarely ever listen to what our bodies are truly asking for, or truly need, whether that's to move more frequently when we are working, or to do slower, more soothing exercise that will help calm our nervous system.

At points in my life, I have been completely deaf to anything my body was trying to tell me. In my twenties, I sat for hours, pushing myself mentally at work, my nervous system on overdrive. I'd rush around after things I thought would give me meaning. I've always known the importance of moving my body to keep it healthy, but during this period of my life, everything was intense – and fast! There was nothing slow, nurturing or soothing about my life and eventually my body began to let me know that both my mental and physical worlds were out of balance.

My life of boom and bust – sitting too long, putting pressure on certain parts of my body, followed by spurts of high-intensity movement – ultimately created high stress in my emotional and mental life. And when I pushed myself too far, my body would resort to giving me a physical signal, usually a stye in the corner of my eye. It took me a while to even connect that these styes only visited me when I was stressed and exhausted.

The body can do weird and wonderful things when it wants to, things we often don't understand. When we're unaware of what causes physical symptoms, we often begin to question our bodies, becoming frustrated or angry with them, maybe even adding to our mental stress or anxiety. Now, when I feel the beginnings of a stye, that's my cue – a gift from my body, telling me to slow down or find a few more minutes a day to meditate. More often than not, rolling out my yoga mat, instead of heading to the gym, will stop that stye in its tracks – and leave me feeling a lot more grounded. Simply paying attention to your body more, in a passive and unbiased way, can allow you to begin to see links between physical body signals and internal messages. You don't need to go looking for solutions, or even get caught up in the 'whys' for now. Just beginning to listen to what your body is telling you is the key to building that conversation.

Body wisdom

Through my practice of Wellfulness, I've discovered a few things about my body. When I go through big changes, or I have to perform in an important meeting or prove my skills in an assessment, my digestive system goes haywire. I find it difficult to digest normal meals, I bloat and get an upset stomach. When I don't get enough light and fresh air, my arms go dry and scaly with eczema. When I'm stressed and feel out of control about a situation, I'll clench my teeth in my sleep and give myself headaches. When my diet is off and my physical energy stagnates, my tongue swells slightly and my teeth make painful indents into it.

When you tap into how you feel in your body, you will get information back from it that informs you how to respond. If I'm listening to my body while I work, rather than just focusing on the limited perspective of my mind, I notice when my back begins to ache, my head starts to throb and my eyes begin to sting. I now take that information as a signal to take a break, get away from my screen, take a walk and get some air, rather than pushing onwards regardless of how I'm feeling. I never regret these breaks, coming back to my desk clear-headed and more productive.

This is a wonderful example of the mind-body connection – the body signalling that the mind needs to rest. Of course, when I'm really engrossed in work, I can still find it difficult to honour this connection. But ultimately if you create a strong sense of interoceptive awareness and listen to the messages you receive from your body, you will have greater ability to respond in appropriate and adaptive ways – rather than react, for example, by pushing yourself too far in another direction, or worse not receiving the messages at all.

When your body is not being listened to on the inside, through the internal interoception signals it sends you, it often resorts to grabbing your attention on the outside. Imbalance, mental stress or anxiety all show up in different ways for different people. One great example is being slightly dehydrated, which can cause headaches, tiredness, dry skin and more – all messages from your body to drink more water! When we do, we have more energy, a clear mind, a fresher complexion, maybe less bloating. We forget how good it feels to give our bodies what they need, because we are so used to living in a state of mild physical imbalance. What signals is your body screaming out for you to hear?

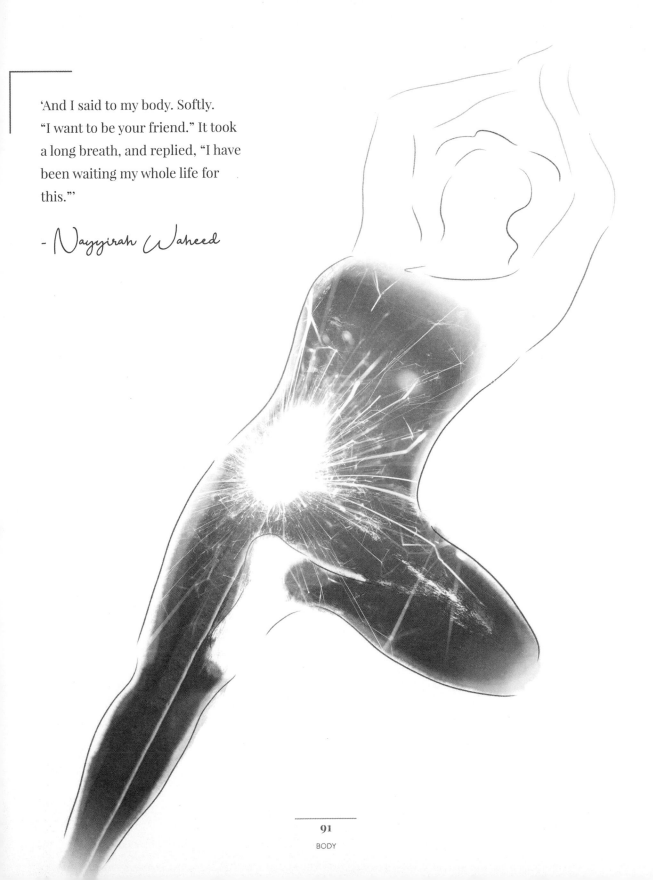

'And I said to my body. Softly.
"I want to be your friend." It took
a long breath, and replied, "I have
been waiting my whole life for
this.'"

— Nayyirah Waheed

Do you want to get to know your body more and really hear what it's telling you? This meditation is a brilliant tool to not only develop mindful thinking, but also to develop your sense of interoception and hear the messages your body is sending you. This is one of my favourite meditations; I always feel completely blissed out after it (or I fall asleep – in fact, it's a beautiful meditation to use for sleep to get you out of your head if you're a lights-out worrier!)

one

Lie down on the floor or your bed. Really look after yourself – use blankets, pillows and even an eye mask if you wish. I love to put two big pillows under each knee and, if I'm feeling really crazy or stressed, even a cushion under each arm.

two

Close your eyes and bring your awareness to your body as a whole. Feel the points at which it touches the ground or bed and get that sense of gravity holding you in place.

three

Now, bring your awareness to the top of your head. What sensations do you feel there? Be really curious. What do you notice? What do you feel? Just observe what comes up. Do you notice unpleasant or pleasant feelings? Perhaps you can't feel any sensations at all. Whatever you notice, simply allow yourself to feel it's there, not trying to push it away or embrace it – just gently and non-judgementally being with the sensation.

four

Now move down to your face and neck, again noticing any sensations – perhaps the soft feel of your collar or an itch on your nose or lips.

five

Gradually move down your body, to your shoulders, arms, hands, then chest, taking some time to feel the sensation of your breath there. Move down into your belly as the breath travels down, then to your hips, thighs, knees, calves, ankles, feet and toes, stopping briefly at each part to notice any sensations. Keep your attention with your body and not with the stories or judgements attached to these sensations. Practise just being with the pleasant and the unpleasant sensations – the positive and the negative – and allow yourself to be interested and curious in what you find.

six

Once you have scanned all of your body, being as detailed as you wish, bring your awareness back to your body as a whole, before gently rolling to one side and taking a moment before sitting up.

seven

It can be helpful to spend a few moments after this meditation to write down or discuss what you've discovered. You might find answering these questions useful:

☐ How did it feel?

☐ Where do any feelings you had live in your body?

☐ What did you notice?

☐ Did you hear any messages your body was trying to give you?

☐ Did you stay with your body or did your mind wander? (This is normal and happens to all of us.)

☐ If your mind wandered, what happened when you realized your attention was no longer on your body? Did you judge yourself or come back to the meditation, showing kindness towards yourself?

The importance of movement

Many people would count exercise as playing a huge part in taking care of themselves, whether they're looking to lose weight, have fun or just feel great. But for exercise to make a real difference, it needs to be a long-term part of your life that you remain excited by. It must not only make you fitter and healthier, so that you feel great in your body, it must also make you feel great in your mind and heart, so that you want to do it again and again. In this way, you create real habits that fit into your lifestyle and work with you, so that they become something that nourishes every part of you. In my experience, when exercise doesn't nourish your body, mind and heart, you either give it up, or worse, it becomes a punishment – a source of discomfort, suffering and dread. You start finding excuses not to do it.

Because society often tells us that we should exercise in order to be healthy, there can be a narrative around it – in order for exercise to be good for you, it has to be hard work and therefore unenjoyable! But, if this is your perspective, what if you could change it so that you love exercise? Through practising Wellfulness, you can not only cultivate awareness around which exercise works for your body, mind and heart, but also around the stories you tell yourself about it and why you do it. When you realize that you have a story on repeat that doesn't serve you, you can decide to consciously change it. You can change how you exercise and how you think about it, and begin to take back control, choosing a type of exercise as part of a wellness plan that works for you.

BODY

It's okay to change your mind

Netball was a huge part of my life when I was at school and university. I loved the game, the skill, the team spirit and the feeling of playing. When I left university, I joined an adult-league team, but, a few months later, I dislocated my ankle. After numerous hospital trips, X-rays and scans, it took months to get back to netball. Then I discovered that being off out of the game for so long had changed the way I saw it. My heart just wasn't in it any more. It took a long time to accept this. Netball had become a part of who I was and even some friends struggled with the fact that I was no longer playing. But with time, and that vital ingredient of compassion, I discovered that it was okay to change my mind – okay for netball and I to part company. It was the start of a new era for me. We are transient, ever-changing beings and that is our right! Change allows us to grow, and I'm now very conscious of allowing change to happen more naturally, noting any resistance I feel as an opportunity to explore and learn more about myself.

Sometimes, even though we don't consciously create change in our lives, it happens anyway. One of the most valuable lessons I've learned through mindfulness, is that allowing myself and others to be who and where we are is one of the greatest gifts we can give ourselves. It takes a great deal of awareness and compassion, but this is what leads us to the liberation of acceptance. Acceptance is so freeing, and it has allowed me to change and grow without guilt, to become the person I am now. I will change my mind again and again and again. It's part of what makes life so beautiful and varied.

There are so many ways to exercise and move our bodies, but you should never be defined by the exercise you do. You are so much more than someone who 'does yoga' or 'plays netball' or is 'into hiking'. One of my teachers always reminds us that we often imprison ourselves inside a glass box of our own making. I imprisoned myself by telling myself that netball was who I was, and that without it, I would be less me, even though I knew it didn't serve me any more. Do you want to smash through your glass cage? Acceptance is the tool with which you can break that glass and liberate yourself to live more fully. Look for the spots where you feel resistance to change and apply a soothing balm of kindness to them.

IGNORANCE AND AWARENESS

The Sanskrit word *avidya* (ignorance) is used to describe having a closed mind, a belief that only one way or one perspective is true – it is our unawareness or lack of curiosity. It stops us from living fully and freely and prevents us from creating a positive transformation, because we fail to see what needs to be changed. It also stops us from accepting the things we can't change. It holds us back from growing spiritually and mentally. In the case of Wellfulness, avidya is not knowing what we do or why we really do it; from our inability to see why we spend time with certain people or why we do the job we do to why we regularly tell ourselves that we aren't good enough or that we can't achieve a particular goal.

Another Sanskrit word that appears in yogic philosophy is *purusa* (that which sees), which is often described as the source of awareness. *Purusa* is constant and does not change. It is curious. It opens up things and investigates. It finds the truth. Picture a river. When you are swimming in the river, it is hard to see its current because you are moving with the water. But when you head back to land and watch the river from its banks, you can more easily see the speed and direction in which it flows. This is purusa – the place from which you can see, through observation. *Avidya* is like swimming in the river.

Yoga, mindfulness and meditation will all allow you to begin to spend more time on the banks of the river and less time in the river itself. It takes practice, however. The body and mind are primed for habit and this includes habitual ways of perceiving life and the things we do.

Shifting perspective

Whatever type of exercise or movement you're into, there will probably be a level of physical discomfort involved at some point. All animals, including humans, are designed to move away from discomfort and pain, whether mental or physical, so it's no surprise that we can find ourselves procrastinating about exercise when we know it hurts. But creating a change or reaching a goal almost always calls for some transformative action. I love to practise yoga, but I sometimes find the poses are difficult physically or uncomfortable – even scary – mentally. Yoga brings joy to my heart and health to my body, but the physical discomfort it can cause could have become an obstacle in my mind, a reason for not doing it.

Had I decided to stop practising yoga, because of the obstacles that physical discomfort caused in my body and mind, I would have missed out on so much joy in my heart, as well as a huge physical transformation, including gaining a stronger, more flexible body and the fading of terrible pain in my lower back. Would the exclusion of yoga have served me and my wellbeing in body, mind and heart? Would it have been a positive change to my wellness plan? I know in my bones, the answer is no.

So how do we get past the physical discomfort that holds us back from practices that we know nourish and serve us? Mindfulness would ask us to notice the discomfort and to practise being with it – not trying to change it but allowing it just to be there, sending kindness to ourselves in order to begin to accept its presence as something we cannot control. And this conscious acceptance has a huge role to play around the things we cannot change. In positive psychology, reframing our perspective can help us turn negative thoughts into positive ones. Instead of being put off by or trying to change the physical discomfort we may experience during exercise, seeing it from another, more positive perspective can change our experience of it, so that we can embrace exercise more fully into our wellness plan.

The concept of tapas, from yogic philosophy, really changed my perspective when it came to discomfort with any of the tools or practices I was using to try and grow as a person or improve my life. It refers to a form of heat or fire that transforms or burns off impurities and is often translated as self-discipline.

Tapas is needed in any transformation. When I applied it to exercise, I began to see that the discomfort I sometimes experienced with yoga was not something to shy away from, but something that was necessary to bring change and therefore bring me closer to the better, fuller life I wanted to create through my wellness practices.

More than that, I began to lean into it, seeing it as a sign or proof that I was changing. Tapas is not about suffering or punishment, but actually about the acceptance of discomfort that will, in return, bring health and happiness. When we accept the discomfort that we sometimes feel in exercise – or in any practice in pursuit of a healthier, freer and fuller life – we can reframe it as something to seek out and welcome, rather than push away, avoid or dread.

So if you find yourself struggling with exercise and its place in your Wellfulness plan, I invite you to do some work here – to find a sense of awareness around your inner narrative and habitual perspective. Observe and be curious about the stories you are telling yourself, or what you are deciding to believe is true for you. You can then identify where you might need to practise some acceptance or reframe your thinking to form a more positive perspective, which allows you to begin to see exercise as something you want to do, accepting some discomfort as part of it.

A holistically healthy lifestyle includes exercise as a tool to enhance physical and mental wellbeing. Once you realize that you want exercise to be a part of your life, because you want to be healthy, then and only then can you bring a sense of curiosity to how it serves your needs in body, mind and heart, using Wellfulness. From this place, you can discover what works for you, try new things, let go of the practices that don't serve you, embrace new ones that do, and begin to create a truly holistic wellness plan that is unique to you.

A home for your emotions

Have you ever thought about whether emotions are in your mind or if they are in your body? Think about someone you love – bring them to your mind and see them smiling at you. What emotions do you feel? Do you notice where you feel those emotions in your body? Now think back to the last time you were angry. Where did you feel that in your body?

We live so much from the perspective of the mind's chatter, that we usually don't pay attention to how emotion makes our bodies feel. Also, the physical feeling attached to certain emotions can feel so uncomfortable that we'll do anything we can to push them away or ignore them. We get caught up in the stories attached to our emotions and start overthinking – 'I'm sad because my boyfriend broke up with me and now I know I'll be alone forever…' or 'My work is making me feel stressed, I can't deal with it any more…' Less often, we experience emotions that are caused by physical sensations, such as when shortness of breath at high altitude or in a stuffy room leads to a feeling of panic. Often, we don't consciously understand why we're feeling the way we do.

Yet there's a lot to be said for both feeling and understanding our emotions, because emotions are different to thoughts. Could it be that our emotions are actually physical and the words we attach to them in ours minds – calm, happy, anxious, excited, worried – are just labels to help our minds organize and understand them? Psychologists have debated the chicken and egg theory around emotions – do they begin in the mind, the brain or the body? Do we have to think about our situation before we feel an emotion? Or does our body react to our situation and we then interpret the feeling in the mind?

It is of course helpful to identify how you feel. Essentially, that is what this book is about – identifying and analysing how the things you do make you feel. The human mind was built to analyse and think. But when we live our life solely by the mind's interpretation of the world, without awareness around the perspective of the body and of the heart as well, we can create imbalance in our physical and mental health through the choices we make and the way we live.

101

BODY

A life lived only according to the reason of the mind is an unauthentic one, because we neglect the two other elements we experience the world through – body and heart. In which case, could paying attention to the physical sensations that emotions create in your body not only help you understand those emotions, but also deal with them more efficiently?

After the Bodyscan meditation practice (see page 92), you were asked to consider some questions, including 'How did it feel?' and 'Where do any feelings you had live in your body?' Mindfulness practice often asks you to focus on the sensations you are feeling in your body, as that anchors you more in the present moment. This can be helpful, not only because you are practising listening to what your body is telling you in terms of physical health, but because it means you begin to disconnect from the stories you attach to your emotions, which can greatly improve your mental health.

EXPLORING WELLFULNESS

When we get caught up in why we feel sad, or anxious or stressed, we often try to fix the thing you think is causing us to feel this way in the first place. In some cases, we can consciously change our situation, but when we can't control or change something, for example, when an injury means you can't run a marathon you've trained for or an aggressive work colleague is making your life hell, trying to fix or control it can actually lead to more stress or emotion, making you feel even worse.

In yogic philosophy, it isn't debated where emotions live or where they originate, only how to find less fluctuation between them, so that life feels less like a dinghy riding the waves of an angry ocean, and more like a steady ship on the gently rolling sea. How? You guessed it – by focus and awareness through meditation.

In Buddhism, it is suggested that to free yourself from that rollercoaster feeling that emotions can cause, you must first acknowledge that you cannot always control the situations causing our emotions – good or bad – but that you can control your reactions to them. By not judging or labelling your emotions as good or bad, pleasant or unpleasant, you stop yourself from getting caught up in their stories, and allow yourself, by simply acknowledging they are there, to let them pass, which they inevitably will, as all emotions are transient.

To sum up, by focusing on where you feel an emotion physically, you don't ignore it or push it away, but you don't get caught up in the stories that can make you feel worse. You can then find that it feels more manageable to just be with the emotion and, by sending kindness and compassion to yourself, acceptance of the emotion becomes possible. You can then allow it to be there, without the internal battle that causes you so much added discomfort. We'll touch on this more in the Mind chapter (see page 168).

A Wellness Practice

BEING WITH YOUR EMOTIONS: A MEDITATION

Your body experiences emotions in a different way to your mind, but so often the mind's stories can be so loud that we miss what the body experiences. Here we will learn how to listen in a deeper way to the body, and interpret the physical sensations of emotion. This might be a tough meditation if you are suffering deeply, so be kind to yourself and ease off if you need to.

one

Find a quiet space, without any distractions, to sit down and settle comfortably. If it feels okay, close
your eyes.

two

Think of a situation you are feeling uncomfortable about in your life. It can be anything, but try to choose something that is not too difficult for you to think about right now.

three

Take a few calming breaths, and then bring the situation to mind. How do you feel? Try and keep your attention focused on your body. Don't focus on why you feel the way you do or any stories attached to your feelings. Just stay with what your emotions make your body feel. Where do they live in your body? Where can you feel them?

four

What are these feelings like? Pleasant or unpleasant? Soft or hard? Steady or moving? Be curious.

five

Try not to judge them, tell yourself off or change them by pushing them away or grasping onto them tighter. Simply observe them and stay with the physical feelings.

six

If you find this uncomfortable or your mind wanders – that's okay. Use your breath to come back to your body. Simply stay there for a few moments, allowing yourself to just be with your feelings, knowing you can stop any time you like.

seven

When you are ready, send yourself a wish of kindness such as, 'May I be safe' or 'May I be well' and come back to your breath again and open your eyes.

eight

How was that? Think about what it was like to be with your emotions and what you felt in your body for a few moments.

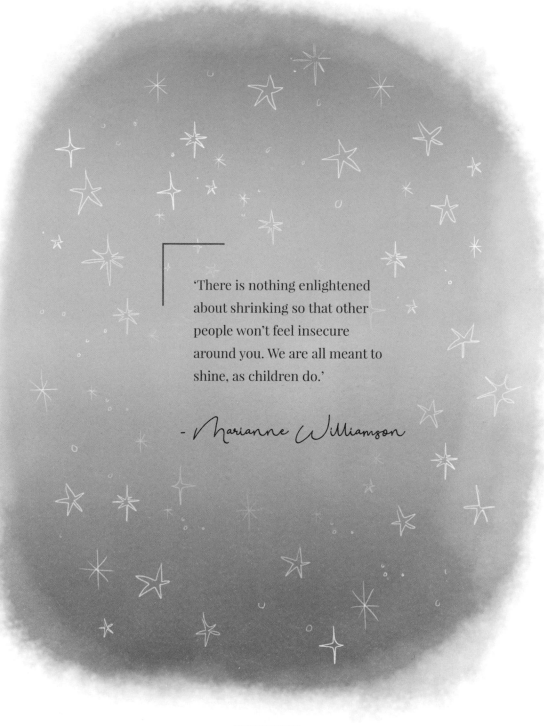

'There is nothing enlightened about shrinking so that other people won't feel insecure around you. We are all meant to shine, as children do.'

– *Marianne Williamson*

Giving your body back control

Have you ever watched children when a song they like comes on the radio or TV – that dance they do, the one with no rules or choreographed moves, where they basically just jump around, arms and legs flying in all directions, with a huge smile on their faces? To this day, my sister and I call this 'Dance how you wanna!' Until a couple of years ago, I hadn't danced like that since I was a teenager. That was until a friend invited me to a retreat in Spain, which included free-movement sessions. The premise is this:

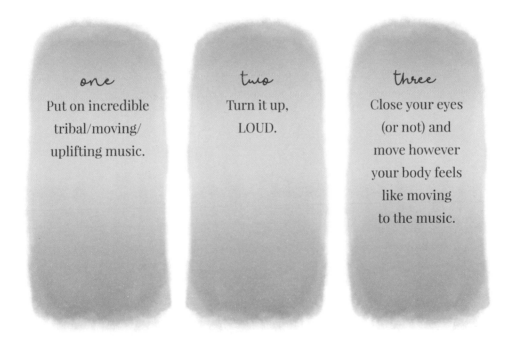

one

Put on incredible tribal/moving/ uplifting music.

two

Turn it up, LOUD.

three

Close your eyes (or not) and move however your body feels like moving to the music.

She played some incredibly moving music very loudly, then asked us to close our eyes (or not) and move around however the music inspired us to. It was a great way to see just how much control our minds have over our bodies – and thoughts and bodies can really butt heads sometimes!

I remember during one free-movement session, gently dancing around with my eyes closed, several minutes in and enjoying the music, that I started to become completely paranoid. I began to imagine my friend was laughing at me. My mind started telling me to stop, to dance less noticeably, to be less free and expressive with my body and to live this experience in a smaller way. Eventually my paranoia got the better of me and I opened my eyes briefly to see my friend, eyes closed, arms wide, with a beaming smile on her face, her body moving freely around the room – completely with us all in that moment. I realized then how much of a hold my mind had over my body, how it not only shouted louder for my attention, but also shackled up my body, trying to make it smaller, less conspicuous and give it less control so that it couldn't embarrass me or break any societal rules, which a part of my mind was obviously so attached to.

So I closed my eyes again and began to feel my body take charge. My mind had been proved wrong. All its worries and fears dissolved as soon as I opened my eyes to see that what I thought was a big, bad monster, about to take me down, wasn't there at all. I danced and danced and danced. I shook out my body, freeing it from its fetters, reaching in and pulling the negativity, worry and fear out of it. I was living bigger. Being ME!

A Wellness Practice
DANCE HOW YOU WANNA: AN ACTIVITY

Not all meditation needs to be quiet – we can use music and movement as a basis for concentrating the mind and listening in to the body. This is a joy-filled practice – but it might not always be easy! Try to smile as you dance, to bring a sense of playfulness to dissipate any worry, judgement or embarrassment you might feel. Let go, smile, and dance, sister, dance!

one

Find a space, where you can have some time to yourself. Check in with how you feel, or how you would like to feel, and choose some mood-lifting music to play.

two

Do what you need to do to feel safe and separated from distraction. Draw any curtains or close any blinds or shutters. Turn off your phone, tablet or computer, if you need to. Perhaps close your eyes. I like to close mine to stay tuned into my body more, as visual stimulation can be distracting.

three

Put on the music – LOUD! – and DANCE HOW YOU WANNA! Tune into your body and let it do what it wants to do. Can you let it move how it wants to move, instead of thinking about it too much? It doesn't matter what you look like, only how you feel. There are no rules!

four

As you dance, stay curious about how you feel. Where do your feelings live in your body? If you feel silly, that's okay. Breathe in compassion, breathe out love towards yourself for trying this practice and breathe into any discomfort. You don't need to fix this discomfort – just notice it, be interested and curious about it – 'Oh, I'm feeling stupid! I want to laugh at myself! That's interesting.' Whatever you feel, whether joyful or sad, allow your body to move you through your emotions as you breathe into them. Maybe they will pass, maybe they won't – it's okay either way!

five

When the music stops, stand, sit or lie still. Bring your focus to your breath and to your body. What sensations or emotions do you feel now? If you feel any emotions (which is very common in this practice), stay with them and try not to push them away. Ask, 'Where does this emotion live in my body?' Be curious, non-judgemental and simply observe.

six

Once you have spent a few moments exploring this practice, either mentally or using the Wheels of Wellfulness tool (see page 42), ask how it made you feel in your body, your mind and your heart. Ask how it served you and if you feel this practice will be a nourishing habit to add to your wellness plan.

Body image

At this point in your Wellfulness project, it's important not only to look at the health of your physical body, but also at the health of your mind when it comes to how you perceive your body image. In a study that really shocked me, researchers suggested that the greater dissatisfaction women feel towards their bodies than men could help to explain why women suffer more from depression. Many studies have researched why negative body image effects so many of us, with societal pressures via the media cited as the main contributor to why we dislike the bodies we were born in. I struggled with negative body image for many years and, if I'm honest, it's something I will probably have to work with on some level forever.

After being bullied for being chubby as a child, I spent much of my teens and early twenties trying to lose weight to look 'perfect' through various forms of unenjoyable, restrictive diets and arduous workout plans. I'd write lists of rules for myself – things I couldn't do and things I must do. It doesn't sound very kind, does it? It didn't feel kind either – it felt like punishment, which is not surprising as it came from a place of shame, embarrassment and often hatred towards my body. But, through my Wellfulness journey, I became aware of the lack of kindness I practised towards myself and how this was causing me so much more suffering. My new wellful way of treating my body required love. I began to hear what my body needed to be truly healthy. I started to feel so much better, not just physically, but in my mind and heart, too.

I discovered that often, without even realizing, I was trying to change so many parts of myself that could not be changed. Naturally, I have dark, curly hair, which is often unruly and wild. It was also excruciatingly uncool when I was at school, and it was even more fodder for the bullies. I was so hurt and alone that I did anything I could to fit in. I remember the day I got my first pair of hair straighteners. I came into school the next day with my hair long, sleek and straight and, although I know it sounds vacuous, it changed my life. The girls who had bullied me suddenly wanted to talk to me. Boys started being nice to me. I learned something that day – straight hair equals acceptance – and I didn't stop straightening it for the next 12 years. And yet my curls never really submitted to the brutal heat. After every wash, they would spring back, reminding me of the exclusion and pain of being bullied.

As the shame of being bullied returned every time my hair was curly, shunning the way I naturally looked took its toll on me. This was an uncomfortable truth, and one I avoided acknowledging until only recently, because it was too uncomfortable to sit with and pay attention to. But as I became more aware of how I was living my life and as I tried to live in greater alignment with not only my mind, but my body, heart and values, I became very aware of my shame and the habitual perspective I had on how I looked. I started to understand that my efforts to 'fix' my hair and force it to fit in were small acts of violence to myself by repeatedly telling myself that the way I looked naturally was not good enough. I can straighten my hair temporarily, but I can never truly change it. It is curly, big and wild and always will be. Unless I accepted that and let go of my shame, I would forever be a creator of my own suffering.

Through focused awareness, using the practices described in this book, I've slowly but surely moved away from punishing and pushing myself to look a certain way and towards listening to my body, nurturing it and allowing it to tell me what it truly needs. In turn, my body is stronger, leaner and healthier than any other time in my life. This has led to a strong relationship with my body, based on what all healthy relationships thrive on – respect and acceptance. I began to trust it and allow it to simply be as it is.

Of course, I still work towards improving aspects of my physical health and other elements of my life where I can, but conscious change could only come after I found that magical equation of mindfulness: non-judgmental awareness + kindness + compassion = acceptance.

Acceptance around your body image is one of the most difficult things you can work towards, using this book. So if you are struggling with it, breathe in a sense of kindness towards yourself, however small. Maybe you could come back to this issue once you've cultivated a greater sense of acceptance with other areas of your life. The point here is to put your wellbeing first. My body image has hugely improved since I was in my early twenties, but I still have a few hang-ups, old and new. Tread slowly, this is a long journey, not a short sprint.

BODY

A Wellness Practice

This is a practice for self-study and mind-body connection. I call this a 'mirror practice' as it has the power to hold up a mirror to your internal world. It has been designed to help you look within and get curious about how you are feeling – not how you should be feeling or how someone else wants you to feel.

Yin yoga works with the body's connective tissue and can be great at relieving tension in areas that often tighten when we suffer emotionally or from high stress, but it can also be tough emotionally, especially if you are struggling with a highly emotional situation, such as grief. So, as always, practise self-compassion and don't push yourself too hard. Remember also that every day is different and that you are unique. The practice might feel different each time you do it and you might have a different response to it than other people. There is no one size fits all.

When doing this practice, stay with it and get curious. I often want to push a pose and the sensations I feel from it away from me. I find this depth of experience so interesting. At other times, I find myself wrapped up in a story or thoughts linked to the emotional reaction I'm having to the pose. For example, in frog pose, I can feel angry and start thinking about things that annoy me. In sleeping swan, I've felt sometimes a peaceful sadness. I might also feel happy sensations or think pleasant thoughts, which are, of course, easier to sit with. But exploring the unpleasant thoughts and sensations is a great way to get curious about yourself, study your mind and, in a simple way, practise the concept of being more interested in the things you do in life, which is the first step of Wellfulness.

one

Grab a watch or timer. Take a moment to arrive on your mat and check in with how you feel, in your body, mind and heart. Allow whatever comes up to simply move into your awareness, and then let it go.

two

Child's pose (Balasana)

Now start in child's pose with your knees
wide and big toes touching. Take five deep
breaths, filling your belly then your chest,
allowing your ribs to expand from the sides
of your body, through your back. Slowly
breathe out through your nose. You can come
back to this breath and this pose at any
point.

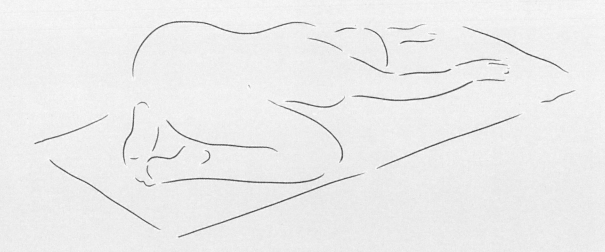

three

Pigeon Pose (Kapotasana)

1. Now place your hands directly underneath your shoulders. Come to downward facing dog briefly, then bring your right knee forwards to place it behind your right wrist. Allow your right ankle to rest over towards your left wrist. Sit your hips down onto the floor. You are now in pigeon pose. Slowly reach your arms forward and lower your forehead to the mat if this feels comfortable. Set your timer and stay in this position for 3 minutes, breathing as before, gently and calmly through your nose.

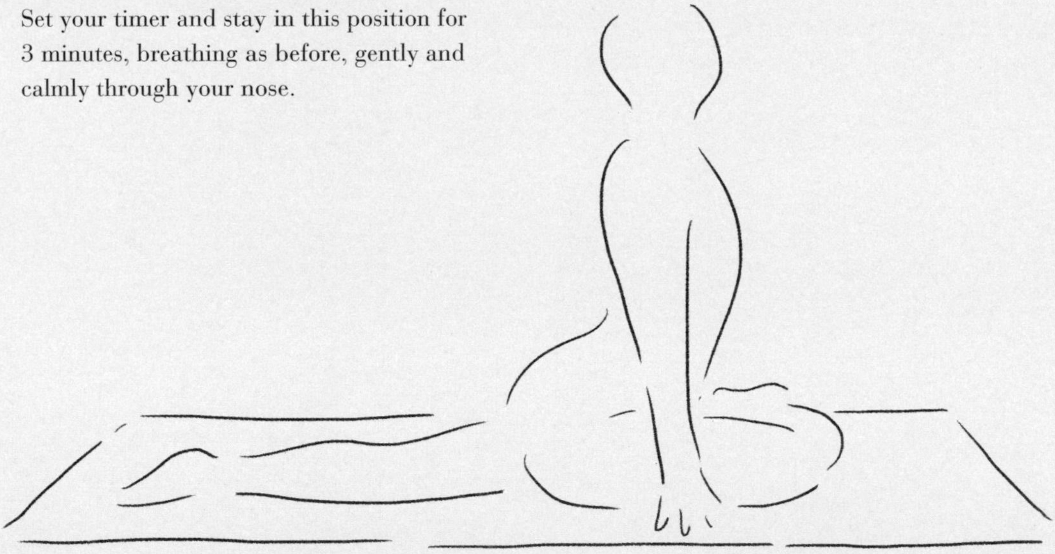

Pigeon Pose (Kapotasana)

2. Check in while doing the pose (and all the other poses to come in this sequence) with your 'hard edges' – any sharp pain or very strong emotional feelings, and your 'soft edges' – slight, although not exactly pleasant, discomfort that you can bear.
If you feel a 'hard edge', it's okay to move away from it and show yourself some compassion, until you come to your 'soft edge'.

Pigeon Pose (Kapotasana)

3. After 3 minutes, switch to the other side, this time bringing your left knee forwards and placing it behind your left wrist with the top of your left ankle over towards your right wrist. Stay in this position for another 3 minutes. You might find that you feel some tension and discomfort, both physically and emotionally, as you begin to work into your connective tissue. This in itself is a strong meditation. You might feel impatient or come up with excuses as to why you should stop. Try to notice this as the feelings arise, and get curious about them. Where do you feel them?

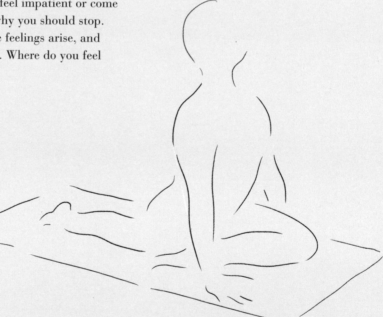

four

Frog (Mandukasana)

Come back to child's pose, bringing your
knees wider than before, and this time
moving your feet wide too so that your feet
are directly behind your knees. You can
either be up on your hands or down on your
forearms. The pose is called the frog. Stay
in it for another 3 minutes, noticing the
thoughts and emotions that come up, and
getting curious about them.

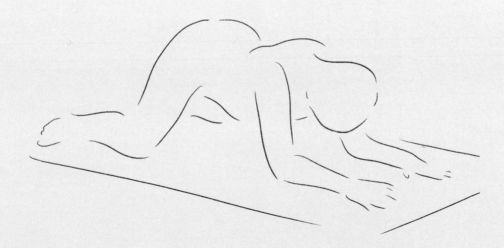

five

Snail (halasana)

Now come onto your back and, using your hands to
support your hips, lift your legs directly up into the
air, and then slowly lower them so that your feet rest
over the top of your head. Your legs can be straight or
bent, depending on how you feel in your body. This
is a deep spinal stretch; be careful to keep your neck
still while you're here. Stay for 1 to 3 minutes.

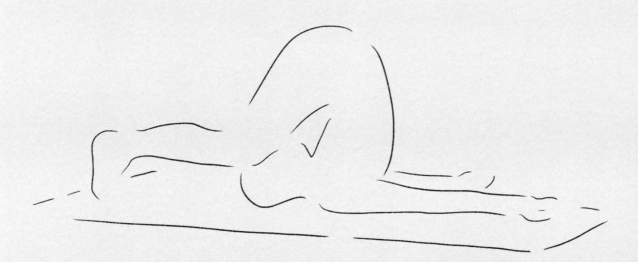

six

Corpse pose (Savasana)

Slowly unfurl and spend a few moments
in savasana by lying flat on your back,
allowing your ankles and feet to relax,
arms out to the side and palms facing up
to the sky. Notice any sensations in your
body, simply observing them and letting
them be, before ending your practice with
three deep inhales through your nose and
exhales through your mouth.

Body Closing Ritual

Now's your opportunity to take a deeper look at your relationship with your body and your physical health. Our bodies and the relationships we have with them are complex to say the least, and this chapter may have uncovered some thoughts or realizations for you about the relationship you have with yours. It also may have revealed some discoveries about how you use your body, how you feel in your body, and what you want to change. This closing ritual will help you to realize where you want to make conscious changes in your physical wellness plan, and begin to accept your body with love where change isn't possible. At the end, you'll have a complete and unique Wellfulness plan for your physical health. Find a sacred space, grab your journal or print out a few Wheels of Wellfulness templates, and settle in.

one

Begin by taking a small breathing-space meditation. Close your eyes and inhale deeply to the count of 4, then hold your breath to the count of 4, then exhale to the count of 4. Pause briefly and repeat for 3–5 breath cycles. Open your eyes.

two

Bring your focus to your body; and then meditate for a few moments on the different ways you use your body each day, from types of exercise you do, when you exercise, if and when you skip or don't exercise, how you use your body day to day – the bags you carry, the shoes you wear, the speed you move at. Even the way you think about your body, and your body image. Focus on how these feel, and be conscious to just stay with the feelings, rather than the stories attached to them.

three

Now consider how each exercise, approach or way you move your body make you feel, in body, mind and heart? How does it serve you? How does it nourish you? Breathe in a sense of wonder around the exercises that feel wonderful, your passions, the things your body allows you to do every day, the practices that feel blissful in your body. Find the joy here! Be curious and playful. Enter each one into the relevant circles, or intersections if they overlap by serving two, or even all three areas of body, mind and heart for you (see an example on page 125).

---

four

Now ask: 'What's not serving me?' What doesn't nourish or serve your body, mind and heart? Place these outside your Wheels of Wellfulness, as I have in the example. Try not to judge these as 'negative', or find ways to change them. Just notice that they exist, and bring those that aren't serving you to mind with a sense of kindness and compassion.

five

Now look at the contents of each circle for body, mind and heart. Everything in the middle intersection, where all three wheels overlap, are the things that serve you fully on a holistic level. Everything outside your wheels are the things that do not serve you. The things that sit within one wheel, are only serving you on a very basic level, and it's your choice as to whether you continue or adapt them to suit you on a more holistic level. The things outside your wheels completely do not serve you, and with this new awareness, you can decide whether to accept them, let them go, or adapt them to meet your needs.

six

It's time to consider the next steps you'll take through conscious acceptance and conscious change. Ask yourself, or journal your answers to the questions below:

☐ Is there anything you need to practice compassionate acceptance around your discoveries? For example, the fact that you realise although you've run most days for five years, it's actually bad for your lower back. Or that until now, you've had a very negative body image.

☐ Now, looking at your wheels, what will you consciously change? For example, you're going try to swim one day a week as it makes you feel relaxed and you love the variety of strokes.

☐ If you feel any resistance to the idea of accepting or changing, simply observe these thoughts and bring back a sense of conscious compassionate acceptance. Can you allow yourself to just observe this resistance and allow it to be? What's that like?

seven

So, taking this all into account, how will you continue to cultivate conscious choices when it comes to your body and the way you move and exercise? How can you use this choice to respond, rather than react and act habitually when it comes to your movement and physical wellness habits? How can you find equanimity and flow here, so that even when stress, emotion, or busyness or temptation hit, you can continue to make mindful choices that serve you and your wellness?

For ultimate Wellfulness in your life, practice asking yourself how you feel in your body, mind and heart for each way you use your body going forward; every new exercise practice you try, each new wellbeing experience you discover. Over time you'll strengthen that mindful muscle that helps you make choices that serve and nourish your body, mind and heart when it comes to exercise, movement and your body.

What doesn't serve me?

BODY

Running: tedious, tiring, doesn't have a huge effect on my physical form – drains my body, mind and heart

———

Lotus pose after an injury

MIND

Comparing my body to the media's stereotypes or other people's bodies

———

Forcing my body via my mind into yoga poses that aren't available to me yet

HEART

Guilt-tripping myself or punishing myself if miss a day

BODY

MIND

HEART

Gentle yoga and
swimming when I'm
feeling fatigued,
HIIT, circuits and
weight training

Feeling of euphoria
after a high intensity
spin class or yoga
practice

Ashtanga yoga –
playful, joyful,
physically demanding

———

Slow kula yoga
(compassion yoga)

———

Sprints and spin

———

Walks/jogs in nature

———

New trends - keeps
me interested!

———

Yoga sequencing
for myself

Gratitude for all
my body can do

———

Body image
affirmations

Trying difficult yoga
poses - learning to
fail well, build confidence
and to practice without
an end destination

Wheels of Wellfulness: My Wellfulness plan for my physical health

Space

There is a whole area of psychology dedicated to the study of our surroundings. It's called environmental psychology and is focused on the relationships we have with the world around us and its affect on us humans. And there's no doubt that it does – psychologist Roger Barker was the first to show, in the 1940s, that we behave differently in different environments and that we also behave uniquely, having different responses and behaviours to other people in the same environment. So how is your environment affecting you? How do you behave in each different space? And how does that shape your health and your happiness?

Sacred spaces

When you think about the spaces that you regularly spend time in, it's likely that you have different spaces for different uses and you'll interpret them all differently. If you love cooking, then it's likely that your kitchen will be well cared for and organized to suit you. If you don't cook much, the kitchen might not have as much thought behind it, because it is not a special place for you. The way your spaces look and feel will reflect the meaning that they have in your life. Another example is your bedroom. Sleeping spaces are usually important to us and we often take time to make them somewhere that we feel safe and cocooned. So where are your meaningful spaces? Where do you spend your time doing things that are important to you and does the way they look and feel reflect this? With some awareness as to how your surroundings make you feel, and the right tools, you can make any space feel special and even sacred.

I worked for a while in a 16th-century barn, which had been converted into an office, surrounded by nature and old beams, away from the noise of sirens and traffic. It sounds dreamy, but unfortunately it wasn't. The building hadn't been converted to a high standard and had no double glazing or insulation. When the wind howled, which it often did, it would blow bits of paper around the building. It would get so cold that I'd sit at my desk with my coat and gloves on. There were only two small windows and it was so dark that when I went outside at lunchtime in search of some air, my eyes were irritated by the bright daylight. On top of that, we had regular rat infestations and myself and a few others developed strange skin allergies. It was cluttered, we had no creative spaces and the whole place was largely uninspiring.

This space did not serve my body, heart or my mind. But what did my wellful awareness tell me I needed? Well, more inspiration, less clutter, more light and fewer rats. What did I need to consciously accept? I loved my job, so had to keep returning to the barn, which meant that I had to find acceptance there and realize that I was making a choice to keep returning. But could I make a conscious change in order to find some way to cultivate greater mental and physical health in my workplace?

With my newfound awareness, I decided that I could make conscious changes in ways that I had power to. I looked at the spaces I loved, such as my yoga studio, my own living room and the small library at the Buddhist centre where I taught, and thought about the small things in these spaces that brought my heart joy – candles, plants, essential oils, books and art. So, for my heart, I brought my own mug, a candle, some roll-on essential oils and a plant into the office and changed the screensaver on my computer to a photo of the amazing view I had enjoyed on my honeymoon. For my body, I brought in natural products to clean my desk and started going out for lunch regularly. For my mind, I threw out any clutter around me and pinned up images to inspire my creativity.

I can't tell you the effect all of this had on my health and happiness at work. I felt more productive, more organized and freer. By consciously accepting that I wanted to keep my job, I understood that I wasn't being made to show up at the barn every day – I was choosing to. And by consciously changing small elements in my environment there, which I had the power to change, I took charge of the wellness of my mind, body and heart in a place that I spent so much time in. This is the power of Wellfulness.

I've carried what I learned in that barn into working as a freelancer from home. My desk is mindfully put together – the colours, plants, crystals, small pieces of art, objects from nature and the view – everything chosen or placed in position for a reason. As I write, I have a large quartz geode on my desktop and a huge amethyst by my feet. Close by are two scented candles, some potted plants, a piece of washed-up coral, some hand cream, a treasured mug and a conker my husband brought home for me from a walk. Whenever I feel my mind getting bored of this space or my body starts to ache from sitting too long, I go to my bustling health club for a change of atmosphere. Sometimes my heart becomes uninspired, so I head to a café for some new energy or move away from work completely and do some inspirational yoga or meditation. We have the power to shape the spaces we spend time in. Even if it's just the addition of a small photograph or plant, a little mindful attention goes a long way.

'Moonlight floods the whole sky from horizon to horizon; How much it can fill your room depends on its windows.'

– Rumi

EXPLORING WELLFULNESS

Cluttered world, cluttered mind?

A study at Princeton University's Neuroscience Institute found that cluttered spaces can operate like a toddler screaming for attention. Clutter diverts our attention, making it more difficult to process information as well as we would in a tranquil, calm space. More importantly, it can affect our mood, making us feel irritable and frustrated, as it drains and exhausts our mental focus. But another scientific study at the University of Minnesota found that being organized isn't always best. It discovered that people who spent time in a messy room came up with significantly more creative ideas than those working in a tidy space. It seems that if creativity is important to you, then being a little messy is probably a good thing! If health is important to you, however, then the same study found that a tidy and organized space is more likely to make you want to eat healthily and 'do good', such as donate money to charity.

What can we do with this information? Science tells us that different environments can cause us to lean into or away from different aspects of ourselves, whether that's putting our health first or being more creative. So what do you want? And where do you want it? Could a clean, organized kitchen and a messy desk at your office work for you? Or, could a cluttered and inspiring kitchen help you to create amazing meals, while a tidy office supports your role at work better?

Yogic philosophy doesn't have a lot more to add. I wonder if that is because space is such a personal thing and we get to know what we need quicker by tuning into ourselves, or because yogic and Buddhist wisdom usually ask us to look inwards and observe the mind, rather than the distractions of the outside world. But one thing yoga does have to offer is the concept, or observance, of sauca (purity or cleanliness). It suggests that in order to clear the way for us to journey on an enlightened path, we must clear our minds of negative thoughts, cleanse and strengthen our bodies by eating healthily and detoxify our spaces so that we stay focused in our minds and shift our energy internally.

You could try using the Wheels of Wellfulness to compare how different spaces – clean and organized or cluttered, messy and even dirty – make you feel. How do they serve you differently? What do you need? What do you have to accept? What can you consciously change? You could also try this with interior design styles too. Which colours and textures serve and nourish you? Which don't?

Before you start this practice, make a list of the main spaces you spend time in, such as your desk in your office, your bedroom, your kitchen or perhaps a local woodland or beach. Maybe you go to a gym or yoga studio a few times a week. Just list any of the places you regularly spend time in. Then draw or print out some Wheels of Wellfulness diagrams (see page 42) for each of these spaces and start to explore your feelings and reactions to them:

one

Choose a few of the spaces on your list and fill out a Wheels of Wellfulness for each of them. How does each space make you feel in body, mind and heart? Remember to just observe at this point. Simply be curious, without judgement, and allow whatever you feel
to come up.

two

Now look at each of these Wheels of Wellfulness diagrams and decide whether each space serves you, by ticking or crossing the relevant intersections. If your space serves you in two areas, you can tick that overlapping intersection. If it serves all three of these intersections, you know your space serves you on a holistic level. Do any of these spaces achieve the golden tick in the middle (like my example on page 46)? If you only get one or two ticks, then this space might need some conscious work! And if any spaces do not achieve any ticks, (like my example of page 44), then this space doesn't serve you on a holistic level. So, can you see any patterns emerging?

three

For your spaces that don't serve all three areas – your body, heart and mind – ask, 'What do I need?' Allow yourself to ask the question and simply observe the thoughts that respond to it. What have you discovered? What do you need to consciously accept? And what can you consciously change? Perhaps one of these spaces is your office and you don't feel inspired by it or like the atmosphere, but you love your job and so accepting that you need to spend time in this space is necessary. Breathe in a sense of compassion towards yourself and then bring your focus onto what you can change in your workspace to make it more inspiring.

four

Now take a look at the Wheels of Wellfulness for your spaces that do have a golden tick in the centre. Can you see a theme or a pattern here? Ask yourself if it is possible to incorporate elements of the spaces that do serve and nourish you on a completely holistic level into the spaces that don't.

'Document the moments you feel most in love with yourself – what you're wearing, who you're around, what you're doing. Recreate and repeat.'

– Warsan Shire

Your second skin

Two years of working in an office, wearing suits and high heels, taught me how powerfully clothes affect our sense of self and who we are. The uniforms we wear embody the institutions that they are designed for. But what happens when a uniform stands for something that you're not? What happens when you dress from a place that is not authentic to you? In my own experience, the uniform I wore for my job in finance masked my understanding of who I was, but it also help me to find my true self – by making me realize what I was not!

The day I quit that job, I vowed to dress only as and for myself – not how society expected me to or, more importantly, how I thought others wanted me to. One of the greatest acts of self-kindness is allowing yourself to be who you truly are. Your clothes and style can either be a second skin, helping you to feel comfortable and live authentically, or make you feel trapped, uncomfortable and misunderstood. So how do your clothes feel on you? You could do a Wheels of Wellfulness audit on your wardrobe? What serves, nourishes and brings you joy in body, mind and heart? And what drains you, feels uncomfortable and fills you with anything other than self-love? What will you let go of and what will you keep?

People in your space

We are social creatures and as much as the media tells us to meditate with our eyes closed, alone on a cushion, or that the idea of flying off to the middle of nowhere on a silent retreat sounds blissful, so often it is connection with others that has the power to truly heal us. I see it on my retreats. At the beginning of a weekend, strangers come together, with lots of shy and nervous energy vibrating from all of them. Slowly, as we move through the weekend and experience eating, talking, sometimes crying and often laughing together, bonds begin to form. Within a day or less, those who were once strangers begin to hug, share secrets and gift acts of kindness to each other. It is such a beautiful thing to see and, although the yoga, mindfulness and Wellfulness plays its part, the connections that are forged, simply by being with like-minded individuals, are very powerful.

Positive social connections have been found not only to increase mental wellbeing and mood, but also to boost physical health. How? A study has shown that one of the mindfulness meditations that I most enjoy teaching (see the 'Loving kindness to others meditation' on page 136) significantly increases positive emotions. These positive emotions increase 'vagal tone', a sign of good physical health, as the vagus nerve connects the brain to the heart and respiratory system. This drives a positive upward spiral of wellbeing, which the study's findings conclude is facilitated 'by people's perceptions of their positive social connections'. So, having people around you who you care about and care about you, increases your physical and mental wellbeing.

LIFE IS EVER CHANGING

The yogic element of space also encompasses sound, which is essentially vibration; an ever-changing movement of energy through the particles around us. So the element of space also allows us to connect with the fact that life is ever changing, transient. From our minute-to-minute thoughts and feelings, to relationships with others and the way we spend our time, working or playing – by nature, whether we like it or not, life will always change, and this can soothe us in difficult times, or might call for acceptance when beautiful parts of life change and we have to let them go.

I love to do this when I'm feeling down or stressed. It also helps me to get back to a place of love, when I'm feeling impatient or frustrated with someone. Or just do it everyday for a dose of wellbeing. It's a guaranteed mood booster! Remember this meditation isn't really about the person you imagine in your pool. It's about finding softness and space in your own self and warmth in your own heart. Cultivating kindness towards others can often be a wonderful first step towards being truly kind and accepting of yourself.

one

Start by getting comfortable in a quiet space that you love being in. Bring your focus to your breath. Breathe deeply and calmly.

two

Now imagine your mind as a pool of still, clear water. Look at it closely and notice the quality of it.

three

Imagine the face of someone you love, reflected back at you from the pool. Bring them into your mind and feel the love in your heart.

four

Imagine dropping a pebble into your pool and, with it, say to your loved one, 'May you be happy.' Drop a few more pebbles with the same wish and allow them to sink to the bottom of the pool. Really feel the intention behind your words. See the person you love smile.

five

Now think of someone who you don't know quite as well or feel indifferent to. This might be a stranger at the bus stop or a cashier at your local supermarket. See whoever you are thinking of in the reflection of your pool, smile, then drop another pebble into your pool, this time with the kind wish, 'May you be well.' Again, as you send this wish, really notice it sink deep into the pool and fill it with that intention.

six

Now, if you have done this meditation a few times and you feel safe doing so, think of someone you feel more negatively towards. It could be an irritating colleague or someone who has hurt you. See this person in the reflection of your pool. Drop in one last pebble, saying, 'May you be happy.' This might be difficult, but focus on sending out kindness, allowing it to soften your heart as you do so.

Toxic relationships

One of the most joyful realizations I've had is that it's okay to say no to things, to say, 'Sorry, that's not for me, but how about this?' Not spending time with people who don't make me feel good or not doing things that I have no interest in, has been liberating. Life is just too short for all of that. I'm all for kindness, but sometimes the kindest thing we can do is to stop pleasing others and be kind to ourselves first. Another aspect of space is the movement and transference of energy, but giving energy to the wrong places or people in our lives can drain us of joy and even effect our health. Studies have found that negative emotions have the power to cause inflammation in the body. Yet, equally, feelings of love and compassion in relationships have the power to help us regulate our emotions, reducing stress and creating positive feelings of security, trust and support.

So, thinking about creating a healthy environment in our lives is also about choosing the things we fill our time with and the people we surround ourselves with carefully. That includes auditing the commitments that no longer serve or nourish us and excluding devices, apps, TV programmes and events that eat up our time and make us feel lesser in some way – stressed, distracted or lonely. And it even includes friends that make you feel drained, sad or not good enough.

Breaking patterns

One of my greatest lessons involved the unveiling of a habitual pattern of mine, which had its roots in my early relationships. I have shared in this book that I was bullied at school. I reacted to that situation by withdrawing into myself, becoming very timid and allowing people to treat me with unkindness. I remember vividly walking home alone one afternoon, when one of the bullies ran up and spat on me. I watched in silence as they walked away laughing. Even well into my teens, the feeling of shame attached to that memory was still raw, I held onto it for years, torturing myself with it.

Eventually, however, I started to create positive social connections and make new friends. By the time I'd made it to sixth form I was outgoing, happy and excelling in life. I thought I'd healed my wounds, grown my confidence and moved past the playground bullies. But, at university, I suddenly found myself once again in a situation where I was being excluded and tormented. And just as I had when I was younger, I retreated into myself, not facing the situation, but passively allowing it to unfold, watching in fear.

After university, a few years went by peacefully. Then, yet again, the same situation of being ignored and feeling rejected cropped up out of the blue. I felt like I'd been hurled back into the school playground. I couldn't believe I was reliving the nightmare as an adult, but this time I didn't withdraw into my pain. I broke down sobbing, asking my husband, why and how this was happening yet again. Why did I repeatedly find myself in this situation? Would this cruel pattern of exclusion and rejection never be over? It's then that I realized that this situation was an echo in my life, a reverberation – and it belonged not to the bullies, but to me.

In yogic thinking, samskaras, or habits, will often repeat themselves – they are patterns. But it is the action that comes as a result of these patterns that truly affects us. As I applied this thinking to my situation, I realized that I was being presented with the same problem over and over again and not resolving it, but dealing with it in exactly the same way, so that I found myself back in the same place every time. Yogic philosophy, however, explains that when we can identify our samskaras and understand them, essentially gaining awareness of our thought and behaviour patterns, this gives us the power of choice to stop the ones that serve us negatively. I now fully believe it is possible to change the perspective we have on many of our problems, in order to deal with them. I decided I owed it to myself to try and change how I perceived situations in which I felt excluded, rejected, hurt and betrayed.

So, what did I do? I practiced kindness towards those I felt were my tormentors and, most importantly, towards myself. Holding onto anger or resentment only caused me more pain. Internally, I directed empathy towards those who I felt were excluding me, acknowledging that they must be feeling pain themselves to act in this way. If necessary, I stopped spending time around their negative energy. I practised simple affirmations of kindness towards them in my mind – 'May you be well. May you be happy.' It was very difficult at first, but I had to protect my mental wellbeing and, with time, I began to feel my pain dissolve.

When I think about it now, so much of the pain I was feeling was of unhealed wounds resurfacing from my childhood. Letting go of the pain, anger and resentment that had tied me to toxic patterns of behaviour for so long, was one of the greatest acts of self-kindness. Through focusing on kindness, I freed myself.

Space Closing Ritual

Looking closely at where, and with who, you spend time and invest your energy, while asking what nourishes you and helps you grow, can be eye-opening. By finding awareness around the big and small things in your life, you'll uncover what is draining you and what is sustaining you.

Remember that this ritual is not just centred around the physical spaces you inhabit and the people in them, but also the work, roles and responsibilities you bring into those spaces. So take time here. In fact, I'd encourage you to make this ritual a life-long practice, as people and situations flow through you life and change. This closing ritual will help you to realize where you want to make conscious changes in your spaces. At the end, you'll have a complete and unique Wellfulness plan for your space. Find a comfortable spot with your journal, or a Wheels of Wellfulness template.

one

Begin by taking a small breathing-space meditation. Close your eyes and inhale. deeply to the count of 4, then hold your breath to the count of 4, then exhale to the count of 4. Pause briefly and repeat for 3–5 breath cycles. Open your eyes.

two

Now think about the spaces you spend time in, the people in your life, your workspace, commute, your colleagues. Be conscious to just stay with your feelings, rather than the stories attached to them, and observe without judgement. You can refer back to any Wheels of Wellfulness diagrams you have used while working through this chapter, if you like.

three

Now consider how certain environments, spaces and activities, such as spending time with a person, your desk space or attending a weekly choir session make you feel, in body, mind and heart? Ask: how does it serve me? How does it nourish me? For example, the park you walk through on the way to work, or the positive energy you feel from your yoga teacher. Enter each one into the relevant circles, or intersections if they overlap by serving two, or even all three areas of body, mind and heart for you.

Breathe in a sense of wonder and find the joy here! Be curious and playful. Enter the ways your spaces serve you into the relevant circles in your Wheels of Wellfulness (see an example on page 145).

four

Now ask: 'What's not serving me?' What doesn't nourish or serve your body, mind and heart? Place these outside your Wheels of Wellfulness, as I have in the example. Try not to judge these as 'negative', or find ways to change them. Just notice that they exist, and bring those that aren't serving you to mind with a sense of kindness and compassion.

five

Now look at the contents of each circle for body, mind and heart. Everything in the middle intersection where all three wheels overlap, are the things that serve you fully on a holistic level. Everything outside your wheels are the things that do not serve you. The things that sit within one wheel, are only serving you on a very basic level, and it's your choice as to whether you continue or adapt them to suit you on a more holistic level. The things outside your wheels completely do not serve you, and with this new awareness, you can decide whether accept them, let them go, or adapt them to they meet your needs. This completed Wheel of Wellfulness is your Space Wellness Plan. Keep it safe – you'll be using it to complete an all-encompassing unique-to-you Wellfulness Plan later.

six

Now it's time to consider the next steps you'll take through conscious acceptance and conscious change. Ask yourself, or journal your answers to the below:

- [ ] Is there anything you need to practice compassionate acceptance around your discoveries? For example, the fact that you realize your office space doesn't serve you, but you love your job, so you aren't going to quit.

- [ ] Now, looking at your wheels, what will you consciously change? For example, you're going to ask to move desks at work nearer the window, and bring in a plant for your desk.

- [ ] If you feel any resistance to the idea of accepting or changing, simply observe these thoughts and bring back a sense of conscious compassionate acceptance. Can you allow yourself to just observe this resistance and allow it to be? What's that like?

seven

Think how you will continue to cultivate conscious choice around your environment. If it helps, come back to asking yourself what you need. Be creative. You might hate your boss and need to spend less time with him, so ask yourself if you could work from home twice a week, which would mean less time around your him? Maybe you could even transfer to another department. If you can identify what it is you need, you can often find a way to do it.

What's not serving me?

BODY	MIND	HEART
Mess/dirt	**Conditional love**	**Disorganized material and physical world**
Physical clutter		
Unkind or toxic people		
Friends who let me down or don't support me with an open heart		

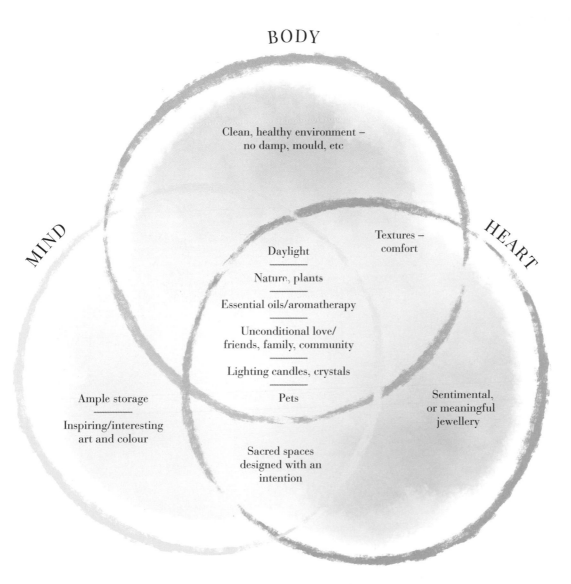

BODY

MIND

HEART

Clean, healthy environment –
no damp, mould, etc

Daylight

Textures –
comfort

Nature, plants

Essential oils/aromatherapy

Unconditional love/
friends, family, community

Lighting candles, crystals

Pets

Ample storage

Inspiring/interesting
art and colour

Sentimental,
or meaningful
jewellery

Sacred spaces
designed with an
intention

Wheels of Wellfulness: my unique Wellfulness plan for my space

Ritual

If I asked you to identify some of the rituals you habitually follow, you might start by thinking that you don't have any. But when you look closely, you'll find that there are rituals everywhere in your life, from blowing out candles on a birthday cake to how you set the table for dinner. From the very meaningful and conscious to the deep-rooted, rituals are an important part of your life. They are a great place to not only learn more about yourself, but also a rich and opulent focus for practising mindfulness and, by doing so, injecting meaning, intention and consciousness into everyday life.

When you begin to apply conscious awareness to your distinctive and individual rituals, you get great insight into the true uniqueness of you. So what are some of your rituals? Bathing? Skincare? Do you have a spiritual ritual? Or do you have a household ritual, such as a particular way of making the bed or washing up? And more importantly, do these rituals nourish or drain you?

A Wellness Practice

GROUNDING RITUAL: A MEDITATION

This is particularly useful in times of stress and anxiety Sometimes, when I have a lot going on in my life, I begin to feel a strange sensation, as though I'm in a hot-air balloon that's become untethered and starts to lift and float aimlessly away, as the fire under it heats up. This is a meditation that I do when I'm so busy that I feel myself drifting and becoming uprooted and, ultimately, unsafe.

You can also try this as a practice of mindful movement, linking your breath to actual steps when walking very slowly around your home and, with each step, feeling gravity pull and hold you close to the floor, grounding yourself.

one

Find a quiet place, with no distractions or anyone needing your attention. This is your time. Place a yoga mat or blanket on the ground. Go outside, if you can, and pick some leaves or flowers to scatter around you. Feel a sense of gratitude and of ahimsa (non-violence), picking the plants with love and thankfulness that you are using nature's beauty to heal yourself. You could also pick up some pretty pebbles or stones or, if you have crystals, bring them into your space. Even a houseplant will work. The idea is to help you connect with nature, to bring the feeling of rooting and grounding into your mind, as you place some of the earth's bounty around your space.

two

Now find a scent which will help ground you to your place on this earth. I love the cleansing smoke of burning Palo Santo wood, as well as the earthy scent of patchouli, which I sometimes dab on the corners of my yoga mat or place in an essential-oil burner. Remind yourself of your intention to reconnect with the earth.

three

Sit or lie on your yoga mat or blanket. Set a timer for 5 minutes or longer if you wish. Close your eyes or, if you feel particularly untethered, keep them open and gaze softly at your physical space.

four

Begin to bring your awareness to the points at which your body meets the ground. Feel the heaviness of your body as you find that connection. Can you begin to sense the pull of gravity, contemplating how it holds and secures you to where you are?

five

Now imagine roots beginning to grow down into the ground from your body, from every point at which your body meets the earth, growing deeper and stronger. Feel that tethering to the earth through these 'roots', holding you securely and safely in this sacred spot.

six

Now bring your awareness to your breath – your constant anchor that is always with you, always accessible, a gateway for you to connect mind and body. Find a steady pace, slowing your breath to the count of 4 on each inhale and exhale, breathing into the depths of your belly, rooting your breath deep down into your body and breathing into the 'roots' you have just set down.

seven

When 5 minutes, or longer, are up, come back to your body very slowly by wiggling your fingers and toes, then rolling onto your right side. Sit up and bring yourself out of the meditation with huge tenderness. Try to keep breathing slowly and deeply as you go into the rest of your day, knowing you can come back to this meditation whenever you wish.

Habits as rituals

There's a difference between habits, routines and rituals. Habits and routines are mindless. Of course, they have a useful place in your life. They can help make more efficient use of your time or serve you, such as the habit or routine of brushing our teeth every morning and evening. However, you can also fall into habitual behaviour that doesn't serve or nourish you, such as eating junk food when you're busy or having a bedtime routine that is stressful, disorganized and, ultimately, stops you from getting a good night's sleep.

Often, because habits or routines are by nature mindless, they are designed not to need your attention. But you can find yourself in a sticky situation when you have a habit or routine that doesn't serve you. When no real attention is being paid to it or how it makes you feel or affects you, it can go on and on without you realizing that it is not really helping you. A stressful bedtime routine, for example, raises your cortisol levels, making it more difficult for you to drift off to sleep. And when it comes to creating a wellness plan that serves you, adopting a calmer and more relaxing bedtime habit or routine offers an abundant gift, as poor sleep has been found to be a huge factor in a number of health issues, including obesity, heart disease and depression.

Your habitual and mindless routines have a great deal of potential power within them, when it comes to enriching or depleting your holistic health. So reviewing your habits in order to enquire and get curious about whether they serve or drain you, and to consider their place in your wellness plan, is an important Wellfulness practice. Imagine if mindless routines, such as getting ready for bed, could become Wellful rituals that have intention, so they serve and nourish you. Think about the kind of life that level of conscious living could create for you.

A Wellness Practice

JOURNAL RITUAL: AN ACTIVITY

Journaling can be a very freeing practice – I love allowing my hand to flow across the page without too much thought, allowing my subconscious to share its inner wisdom. Remember, there's no need to censor or write what you think you should write – this is for you only…

one

Grab a notebook and start writing down answers to any or all of these questions: How do you wake up? What sound wakes you? What is usually the first thing you see on waking? What generally prompts your first thoughts of the day? How do these things serve you? Do they nourish you and improve your emotional, physical and mental wellbeing? Or do they shock, drain or negatively take away from your wellbeing? What is your routine? What do you do habitually and subconsciously, and what is intentional? What do you like to take your time over and what do you rush? What do you need to do as part of your morning routine? What doesn't need doing, but is still intentionally or unintentionally there?

two

Once you've spent some time thinking about and answering some of these questions, fill in a Wheels of Wellfulness diagram (see page 42) for your morning routine as it stands. When you can see what nourishes and serves you in your morning routine, and what doesn't, ask yourself what you need, including what you need to accept stays and what drains you and can therefore be lost.

three

Now it's time to get creative. Look at the things you have to do, but that aren't particularly serving you in a holistic sense. Brushing your teeth, for example, serves your body in the sense that it keeps your mouth healthy, but I'm guessing it doesn't do much for your heart or mind. If you're anything like me, you'll spend the time brushing your teeth thinking about how you didn't get enough sleep or the things you have to do today. But what if you could turn this habitual, mindless routine, into a mindful, nourishing ritual and what might that look like for you?

You could take this time to look in the mirror and remind yourself of an affirmation I like to work on – self-love. The specific thing can change over time, but in essence, I like to take those minutes spent brushing my teeth to meditate and focus on my awareness, and try not to fill the time with anxieties over the past or worries about the future.

Bedtime rituals

For years, I had a mindless bedtime. I'd try to prolong my evening and put off tomorrow by watching more TV, tidying up, checking emails and even using yoga as a procrastination tool not to go to bed. I'd do anything other than get into bed and sleep. Which is ironic, because I love to sleep. In the morning, I'd regularly wake up wishing I could stay in bed and have just one more tap of the snooze button, essentially because I wasn't getting enough sleep.

Then I started to try out a few new things as part of my morning routine, such as waking up a little earlier in order to swim or practise yoga before work. This meant that I had to get my yoga, gym and shower things ready the night before. By adding all this to my nightly routine, bedtimes became particularly frantic. There I'd be, at 11pm, pottering around the kitchen, or on my yoga mat, or playing with our cat or watching 10 minutes more television. Eventually I'd stumble around in the pitch black, trying not to wake my husband, while I packed a clean towel, appropriate outfit and everything I'd need for the next day. By the time I climbed into bed, my mind was spinning with thoughts about the next day. Meanwhile, my husband was completely blissed out with a good 45 minutes or more sleep under his belt than me.

It's important to note that my husband is an early bird and I am a night owl, and that what works for one person might not serve the other. But it's also important to listen to your authentic needs. Applying Wellfulness to how my bedtime routine affected my health and happiness really woke me up to just how unhappy it made me feel and to what I was missing out on – a restful night's sleep, full evenings of relaxation and real switch-off time, plus the great potential that a true bedtime ritual offers.

After completing an audit on my evening and bedtime routine with a Wheels of Wellfulness diagram, just as you did with your morning ritual on page 151, I made some amazing changes. Now I unpack and repack my bags before dinner, allowing the rest of the evening to be completely free. I leave my phone in the kitchen and don't check my emails or social media after 7.30pm. I have a full skincare routine, which I'll also often do before dinner, ritualized with an intention of self-love, self-care and self-respect. Then, before I settle down for sleep, I do one, two or all of these three things – gentle yoga, reading or listening to an audiobook, and I almost always meditate in bed as I drift off. I'll still almost always get into bed after my partner, but my whole routine has now been consciously planned to enhance my happiness health, and to suit my authentic needs.

Of course my bedtime ritual can alter from day to day, depending on the natural flow of life, and I practise acceptance around that. I've found it important not to get too controlling around my rituals. If I don't manage to do any of them, I am conscious not to use that as a weapon against myself – they are there to nourish me. But conscious actions and behaviours around the things we repeat in routines and rituals everyday have been a great source of richness for me when it comes to my wellness plan and enhancing my health in a holistic way.

The breath

I love this quote from David M. Bader – 'Breathe in. Breathe out. Breathe in. Breathe out. Forget this and attaining Enlightenment will be the least of your problems.' You spend most of your day breathing and not needing to think about it, which is great, because not needing to think about how to breathe frees up your attention for lovely things like chatting with friends or watching a film, without worrying about whether you need to inhale or exhale. Imagine if you had to think every time you wanted your heart to beat or to digest your food! If rituals are about placing intention and awareness onto an action, then your moment-to-moment bodily functions are not ritualistic. You cannot consciously control most of your vital organs, but you can control your lungs – and therefore, your breath. In that sense, your breath is the gatekeeper to your mind-body connection and your ability to control it consciously provides you with an opportunity to place ritual and meaning onto it.

But why, and how can we make the breath more mindful? Both ancient Eastern wisdom and modern scientific research has found that self-regulation of the breath is a fantastic tool for self-regulating the mind and body. Controlling the breath allows us to influence other functions of the body, such as heart rate, and also of the mind, such as anxiety. The deliberate use of breath can result in health benefits, such as a reduced risk of dementia, or an enhancement of performance or capability. For example, research has found that inhaling before a task might make us better at it, priming our brains for activity and increasing our attention towards what we are doing .

The breath is seen as a powerful tool in yogic practice and modern science is fast discovering evidence that supports this ancient thinking. We're finding more and more evidence to show that breath has a powerful effect on health, especially of the nervous system, where the breath's influence is profound and immediate. Controlled breath practice in yoga – called pranayama (prana meaning 'life giving energy') is so important that a whole limb, or area of yoga is dedicated to it. In its simplest form, pranayama is just mindful awareness of the breath. Even the simple switch to nasal breathing in pranayama can affect

how we feel and function. For example, creating a conscious slowed inhale and exhale through your nose has been found to make us calmer. This is because the nerves inside the nose respond to the slow nasal breath by firing in a similar rhythm, slowing the brainwaves. We can even find it easier to enter a deep meditative state through slow nasal breathing, rather than breathing at the same rate through our mouths.

There is fascinating evidence to support how controlled breath can influence our health too. One exciting example is the research around the Sudarshan Kriya pranayama practice, which has been found to be beneficial in treating anxiety, stress, depression and even post-traumatic stress disorder. There is also evidence to support that this rhythmic breathing technique can help to alleviate severe depression, even in people who do not respond to other treatments. But in true Wellfulness-Project style, don't just take science's word for it. Live the experience by doing the practice below to discover how pranayama makes you feel.

Alternate nostril breathing, or Nadi Shodana pranayama (energy cleansing breath practice), is easy and can help you to feel relaxed, yet balanced and energized. It's had some inspiring scientific discoveries around it too. It calms the nervous system, making you feel less stressed, reduces blood pressure, improves mental performance and increases your attention span. It can be done before or after yoga, before or after meditation, before bed or on waking, during a break at work, when you are feeling stressed or out of balance, or simply as one of your daily rituals.

one

Sit in a chair or on the floor cross-legged. Make yourself comfortable with blankets and cushions. Think about how you want to feel and allow that intention to be reflected in your space.

two

Bring your focus to your breath as it is and allow yourself to follow it. You don't need to control it now, just place your awareness onto your breath as gently as a butterfly resting on a flower.

three

Once you have settled into your space, take your dominant hand and raise it to your nose.

four

Exhale fully, then pinch both your nostrils to close them.

five

Release the left nostril, but keep the right closed. Breathe in slowly and fully through your left nostril.

six

Now close off the left nostril and release the right. Then exhale through your right nostril.

seven

Keep your right nostril open and breath in again through it.

eight

Close the right nostril and exhale through the left. That's one round of alternate nostril breathing complete: in through the left, out through the right, in through the right, out through the left. Try and do 10 rounds.

nine

Afterwards, bring your attention back to your natural breath and allow yourself to settle. Did you notice any subtle differences – warmth or increased heart rate or any emotional fluctuations? How did it serve you? Could you try it for a week and see if any larger changes present themselves? Then fill in a Wheel of Wellfulness and discover if it's a practice that serves you and that you want to continue, or if it doesn't serve you and you want to let go.

Affirmations

A small ritual, which I like to practise in one form or another every day, is to repeat an affirmation: a small, meaningful phrase or word that you place the energy of your awareness onto through repetition, meditation or simple focus. You might chant it, sing it, repeat it in your head or out loud, or write it down and pin it somewhere you'll see it regularly. Basically, the simple act of placing your awareness onto a thought can make it your truth. The ancient language of Sanskrit has a beautiful word for this – soma, which in essence translates as the flowing of energy through placing your conscious awareness onto someone or something. But there's some interesting science behind this too. By repeating a thought, you strengthen the cognitive connections associated with it in the brain. These cognitive connections become stronger and stronger through a process called cortical thickening, until the thought becomes more habitual, or even a belief. Over time you can rewire your brain, just as you can through practising mindfulness to be more present, kinder, less reactive and less judgemental.

My go-to affirmation is the Sanskrit mantra, 'Lokah samastah sukhino bhavantu', which translates as 'May all beings everywhere be happy and free, and may the thoughts, words and actions of my own life contribute in some way to that happiness and to that freedom for all.'

When I bring my focus to this mantra and check in with the Wheels of Wellfulness (see page 42), my mind feels at ease and without conflict. My heart feels aligned and perhaps, most interestingly, my body feels warm and soothed. This mantra calms my nervous system, particularly if I say it out loud. I can feel my breath start to slow and any tension in my body starts to slip away. This mantra meets me, serves me and nourishes me on every level. I know in my bones that it's good for my wellness, and my Wheel of Wellfulness reflects that by the big tick in the central intersection, where all the circles meet. So is there a mantra, phrase, quote, proverb or even a word that has special meaning for you and creates a physical, cognitive and heartfelt response?

CREATING STILLNESS AND CLARITY

If you've ever wondered why we chant the sound 'Om' after a yoga session, you might be intrigued to discover that this practice is another of those little gems where ancient Eastern wisdom meets Western science. In one study, researchers asked two groups to chant two different sounds and studied their brains while they did this. One group chanted 'Om' and the other chanted the sound 'Sssss'. They found that the group that chanted 'Om' experienced significant deactivation of activity in the amygdala – a part of the brain that sits in the limbic system, where our fight/flight responses live. The same deactivation was not found when the sound 'Sssss' was chanted. To sum up, chanting 'Om' has the ability to reduce anxiety, fear and perceived threat.

In yogic philosophy, 'Om' is seen as the sound of the universe and connects us to something greater than ourselves. When we are troubled or struggling with something, chanting 'Om' and focusing our awareness onto a higher being, or something greater than ourselves, can create stillness and clarity in our minds, allowing us to move away from the confusing stories that can lead to more suffering, which we often attach to. The study concluded that the sound 'Om' creates a vibration that stimulates the vagus nerve, which plays a large role in feeding information between the brain and the workings of the body. In very simple terms, this stimulation has a calming effect on digestion, heart rate and breathing, moving us into a state of 'rest and digest'.

View your rituals with compassion

When I was at university, I'd often stay up late, working into the night. It was when I'd get some of my best work done. I had no distractions and my mind felt more alive and clearer in the dark hours. So, as this book began to form, it was no surprise that I fully allowed myself to succumb to my night-owl tendencies.

Working late into the night, however, raised two issues. Firstly, I was missing several hours of sleep a night. How would that affect me? I found out soon enough. After a while, my mind became fuzzy, my body sluggish and, in my heart, I often longed to be in bed, asleep. So, what did I need? If being a night owl served my creative self, I had to make sure that it wasn't doing myself a disservice elsewhere, especially when it came to my health. This would mean changing my whole sleeping and waking routine. My usual morning exercise had to move to lunchtime, but with the amount of time I was spending at my desk, I actually found myself craving some form of movement midway through my day. The second issue, however, was slightly more difficult to navigate. I work better at night – it serves me – but unfortunately, society usually doesn't agree. Despite studies showing that being an 'owl' or a 'lark' is actually determined by genetics, society champions 'larks' over 'owls', and so feelings of guilt and failure about my late-night schedule started to drift into my mind.

This bring us to what this book is all about – looking within to discover what serves and nourishes you and separating that from what society, your family, friends, partners or any information out there is saying should nourish and serve your needs, skills and who you are. I had to bring a huge dollop of compassion to this realization. We've been conditioned to listen to society's norms and follow them. It's what keeps us functioning in our communities and of course it has its place, but not when it comes at the expense of health, happiness or success. I feel so passionately about this and yet it's probably the most difficult area to practise acceptance around.

Through your Wellfulness project, I invite you to bring a sense of curiosity to society's conditioning, accept it for what it is and then let it go. The specific idea of 'the early bird catches the worm', which society champions, does not serve me. So every night, I try to look at it without judgement, practise acceptance around it and send it off, wrapping myself in a blanket of compassion as I open my laptop and allow my words to flow.

What are you doing that serves society's ideas of right or wrong, good or bad, but doesn't serve or nourish you?

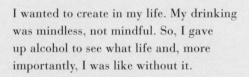

Alcohol has its home in this chapter because, unlike food, we don't need it in order to survive. Yet for so many of us, alcohol can also become a ritualistic habit. We celebrate with it, we unwind with it, sometimes we even like to wallow in it. We use it for many different reasons, such as to feel more confident or to forget negative situations and a million things in between.

After placing more awareness around food and other areas of my life, I realized that I was using alcohol to make me feel less shy and, the older I got, the more that didn't sit right with me. There I was, trying to live more authentically in every way possible, but when a big get-together with friends was arranged, I'd drink to make myself feel bigger, more confident, and more likeable. I felt that I needed to drink just to be interesting enough for my own friends to like me at parties and, sadly, I'd been using the handy gin-and-tonic tool for so long that I hadn't even realized what I was truly using it for. My reasons for drinking were not serving me and the more conscious and aware the rest of my life became, the more inauthentic drinking felt for me and what

I wanted to create in my life. My drinking was mindless, not mindful. So, I gave up alcohol to see what life and, more importantly, I was like without it.

I don't think that there's anything wrong with a healthy and mindful consumption of alcohol. I might drink it again one day, but it will be because I want to experience a specific glass of wine or for a special occasion, rather than using it as a mindless distraction from something uncomfortable or to add a synthetic layer of confidence to my natural self. Removing alcohol from my life to see what social situations are like without it has been a very mindful experience. But aside from using this experiment as a form of self-study, when I enter my life with alcohol into a Wheels of Wellfulness diagram (see page 42) and then my life without it, the two pictures of my life are strikingly different. An alcohol-free life has made my body healthier and happier, my mind less anxious and my heart more joyful by building my confidence and giving me more meaningful experiences.

I've found this topic requires a great deal of compassion, as judgement of ourselves and others can be extreme. When I look back at the way I used alcohol to make me feel, I have so much tenderness and love towards myself. It was as though I was lost at sea, searching for land, grasping at floating islands to make myself feel stable in an unsteady ocean that I felt out of my depth in. I had to take the buoyancy aids off in order to learn how to swim back to land, and now I am home.

Removing alcohol from my life has allowed me to know myself and grow myself. Doing this won't be for everyone, but for me, mindfully choosing not to drink at this point in my life's journey has served me in every way possible. I no longer see any compelling reason to drink in the way that I used to, habitually or ritualistically, that outweighs the impact that being alcohol-free has had on my holistic wellness.

What, if anything, do you rely on in life? Could you practise Wellfulness around it to find more awareness around your relationship with it?

Ritual Closing Ritual

Your ritualistic life might be one you'll need to spend some time with when it comes to creating Wellfulness, feeling it out in your own life and letting ritual begin to find a place in your routine. And there's no need to rush, your life is a universe, there is so much to explore you'll never do it all in one day. So be gentle with yourself, and allow this one come to you. This closing ritual will help you to realize where you want to make conscious changes in your routine, and where you can begin to add meaning and ritual to everyday life.

At the end, you'll have a complete and unique Wellfulness plan for your daily rituals and routines, summing up everything that serves and nourishes you, and opening up new awareness around areas you want to improve on or change to make your life happier, healthier and more aligned to your individual needs. Sit somewhere quiet with your journal or print out a Wheel of Wellfulness template.

one

Begin by taking a small breathing-space meditation. Close your eyes and inhale deeply to the count of 4, then hold your breath to the count of 4, then exhale to the count of four. Pause briefly and repeat for 3–5 breath cycles. Open your eyes.

two

Bring your focus to the routine of your usual day; how you wake, how you dress, eat, travel. Any small habits? A specific snack at a specific time? Lunchtime, evening and bedtime routines too. Focus on how each habit in your day feels, and then on how your routine as a whole makes you feel. Be conscious to just stay with the feelings, rather than the stories judgements you may attach to them. Simply observe your thoughts.

three

Now consider how each ritual or routine makes you feel, body, mind and heart? How does it serve you? How does it nourish you? What about your everyday routine and ritual nourishes your body, mind and heart? And what is working?' Find the joy here! Be curious and playful. Enter each ritual or routine that serves you into the relevant circles, or intersections if they overlap by serving two, or even all three areas of body, mind and heart for you. Start with an important daily routine for all of us, waking, then for any other important routines in your day – bedtime is an important one, but you may have routines which are as unique as you are. Take your time here; as you become more aware, you might begin to see routines and rituals you didn't realise you had! Begin to build a picture of how your mind, body and heart respond to the routines and rituals in your day (you might want to spend just ten minutes here, or make this an ongoing project over the next week or month).

four

Now ask: 'What's not serving me?' What routines have you found that aren't nourishing your body, mind and heart? Place these outside your Wheels of Wellfulness, as I have in the example. Try not to judge these as 'negative', or find ways to change them. You don't have to look for solutions just yet; that will come. Just notice that they exist, and bring each of the routines that aren't serving you to mind with a sense of kindness and compassion. Treat yourself as you would your dearest friend, with love and empathy.

five

Now look at the contents of each circle for body, mind and heart. Everything in the middle intersection where all three wheels overlap, are the things that serve you fully on a holistic level. Everything outside your wheels are the things that do not serve you. The things that sit within one wheel, are only serving you on a very basic level, and it's your choice as to whether you continue or adapt them to suit you on a more holistic level. The things outside your wheels completely do not serve you, and with this new awareness, you can decide whether accept them, let them go, or adapt them to they meet your needs. This completed Wheel of Wellfulness is your Rituals Wellness Plan. Keep it safe – you'll be using it to complete an all-encompassing unique-to-you Wellfulness Plan later in the book.

six

Now it's time to consider the next steps you'll take through conscious acceptance and conscious change. Ask yourself, or journal your answers to the below:

☐ Is there anything you need to practice compassionate acceptance around your discoveries? For example, the fact that you might sabotage your own bedtime by pottering around and getting to bed late every night, which makes you feel tired the next day. You might want to practise acceptance that you are naturally a night owl, with a sense of kindness towards yourself?

☐ Now, looking at your wheels, what will you consciously change? For example, a new ritual of meditating for 10 minutes before bed to calm your busy mind down or getting your bag ready as you arrive home, instead of before bed? How does that decision feel?

☐ If you feel any resistance to the idea of accepting or changing, simply observe these thoughts and bring back a sense of conscious compassionate acceptance. Can you allow yourself to just observe this resistance and allow it to be? What's that like?

seven

So, taking this all into account, how will you continue to cultivate conscious choices when it comes to your routine and ritual? What new rituals will you create, or current meaningless or mindless habits might you attach more meaning to through ritual, be it a moment of mindfulness, of positive self-talk, or a prayer of intention or affirmation? Get curious, and get excited – you're cultivating meaning and isn't that the royal jelly of life?

What's not serving me?

BODY
Using alcohol to make myself feel more confident

MIND
Checking emails at the weekend

———

Looking at my phone as soon as I wake

———

Over-thinking and organizing my next day directly before bed

HEART
Reading the tabloids

———

Self-comparison via Instagram

BODY

Drinking a glass of water
on waking

MIND

HEART

Organizing
tomorrow's bag
before dinner

Bedtime yoga
———
Morning meditation
———
Chanting mantras and singing
———
Setting my sacred space
———
After dinner walks
———
Morning movement
———
Phone-free evenings

Having a plant-
based protein shake
after the gym with
an attached self-
love affirmation

Yoga nidra/mindful
body scan
———
Meditation before bed
when stressed

Journalling
———
Reading before
bed

The use of alcohol to
celebrate or mark an
important moment
with others

Wheels of Wellfulness: my unique Wellfulness plan for my daily rituals

Mind

We can eat healthily, exercise every day, have a beautiful space to live and spend our time in, the most loving and supportive friends and family and a great job, but if our inner world doesn't mirror our outer world, what's the point of any of it? This is a nice moment to come back to your why, which you took some time to consider near the beginning of this book. Why do you want to be healthy? Why do you want to be wellful? For me, it was to live more freely and fully. So, take a moment here to remember your why, and ponder for a moment on how cultivating a healthy mind is important to you.

Over the last few chapters, we've slowly moved from the outside inward, from food and movement of the body to our physical and social space and the rituals we perform. Understanding ourselves – the way we are, the things we do and patterns we repeat – is not an easy thing to do, as you may have found! There may have been some sticky points of resistance in the form of boredom, impatience or rebellion to some of the tools in this book, as you began to dig deeper and find stuff that felt uncomfortable, but that's okay. This is a lifetime's work, so right now, in this moment, breathe in a sense of self-love for being here, for showing up.

Shine your light

Wellfulness helps us understand our habits and how they make us feel in a holistic sense. And if we don't understand the way these habits manifest in the mind, we can live our lives from a place of unconsciousness, ignorance, or even fear. Misunderstandings often lead to reactions that are rooted in fear. There is an analogy that explains this well. When the light is off in a room at night, a long, thin shadow on the floor, in the darkness, could look like a snake. We would probably react by running away, or might try to trap or beat it. It's only if we turn on the light that we are able to see that our 'snake' is actually a harmless piece of rope.

Without the clarity of light, we cannot see the rope for what it truly is and therefore respond inappropriately. Similarly, in the dark shadows of our minds, awareness is the clarifying light. We all deserve to live from this place of clarity, away from the autopilot functioning that so rarely serves us, away from the fear that lives within the pockets of darkness in our minds. Only you can save yourself from this fear. When it comes to living your life to the full, when it comes to fully realizing the potential you are born with, you are your own superhero. That's the opportunity that Wellfulness of mind can bring you.

When you bring the concept of Wellfulness to your mental wellbeing, through practising observation, enquiry and awareness using the Wheels of Wellfulness (see page 42), you turn the light on, allowing yourself to see the habitual ways in which you think and how the quality of those thoughts – negative or positive, limiting or encouraging – is affecting the way you live, feel and experience the world. You will see the thoughts and beliefs that hold you back and the ones that carry you forward. To find freedom from a habitual, reactional mindset, which limits you from living fully and without fear, all you need to do is observe. This simple act of observation enables you to see your beliefs and thoughts for what they truly are and begin to understand them. Real freedom is impossible without understanding.

'As children, we played hide and seek with one another, as adults with ourselves.'

- Yahia Lababidi

But I've got a secret for you... this is what we've been doing all along! Throughout Part 3, we've moved slowly inwards, initially practising Wellfulness in the easier areas of life, from the food we eat and exercise we do, to the space and people around us, and our habitual behaviours; firstly to create a unique wellness plan, but also as a method of learning real mindfulness and all of its concepts, rather than just 'being in the moment'. And now we are able to start finding awareness around the more difficult workings of the mind.

You may have heard the phrase, 'Cells that fire together, wire together', (written by Carla Shatz in reference to the neuropsychologist Donald Hebb's research on learning and the roles that cells in the brain play). So far, we've practiced wellness-related mindfulness over and over, learning how to listen, strengthening our muscle of attention in order to create a habit of awareness around how we feel. We've learned how the things we do affect and create those feelings, and even how we then respond to them.

This brings us back to our neuroplasticity – just like we can train our brains to be more mindful through creating new neural pathways and walking down them in our metaphorical mind forest again and again with each practice, we can also train the brain and create pathways of unhealthy thinking habits, or samskaras. Once the pathways are there it's easy to walk down them repeatedly, leading us repetitively down pathways that may not serve us. But looking at them allows us to see how these pathways don't work for us – they don't serve us or nourish us, and often these pathways don't take us to where we really want to go anyway! We just haven't been paying enough attention to realise. Until now.

So, by this point, you're basically a pro. The only reason we've left this part until last, is because sometimes looking within at the way we think, can be uncomfortable, or even confronting. But don't worry, I've got some tools to help us with that.

ENLIGHTENMENT IS YOUR BIRTHRIGHT

One of my teachers, a Zen Buddhist monk, regularly states, 'You are Buddha.' The first time he said this to me, I was confused. But he explained that 'Buddha' simply means awakened, or the enlightened one. It was a revelation to me that enlightenment was not an impossible feat, reserved for monks meditating in isolation on remote mountain tops. In fact, the word 'enlighten' simply means to 'put light on'. As you shine a 'light' onto your life through the focused awareness of your Wellfulness practice and look within, you awaken to how the choices you're making in your life affect you and how you feel physically, mentally and spiritually. In this way, you become the Buddha, too. Awareness, and therefore enlightenment, is available to all of us. It is your birthright.

Understanding your mind, the ancient way

When it comes to having a healthy mind, what is it that you want to achieve? The most obvious and ultimate goal, for most of us, would be happiness. I mentioned that you are your own superhero when it comes to mental wellbeing, but we all know that the best heroes usually have some obstacles they must overcome in order to find their happy ending. You will encounter obstacles, even tragedies, over your lifetime, from an argument with a friend to losing someone close to you. You cannot stop these things from happening. But mindfulness teaches you how to deal with them in a way that causes you less suffering.

If you've worked your way through this book, you'll know by now that I find yogic philosophy so helpful when it comes to matters of the mind and the heart. In yogic philosophy, a thought that arises in reaction to the things we do or happen to us, is called a *vritti*. Translated from Sanskrit, *vritti* literally means a whirlpool. I think this is such a wonderful word to describe the thoughts and stories that are whipped up by events around us and then whirl around in our minds, often causing mental turbulence or confusion. Think of the effect that a heavy stone has when it is thrown into a pool of still water. The pool is your mind. The stone represents an email from your manager saying that your last report wasn't good enough, or bad news from the doctor on some test results. The whirlpool that occurs, because of the stone being thrown into the pool is your vritti – the emotions and the stories that you attach to your boss's email or the news from your doctor.

The goal of yoga is said to be to gradually quieten any *vritti* you might have, to calm your whirlpool of fluctuating thoughts and mental turbulence, which stems from habits that do not serve you, in order to find peace. You can do this through the practice of simply observing your thoughts without judgement – this is mindfulness.

'All that we are is a result
of what we have thought.'

- Buddha

We're often mislead into thinking meditation is about emptying the mind, but that's really a myth! As you've seen so far, meditation is simply observing. The mind was designed to think, so expecting ourselves to just 'turn off' our thoughts is, well, unrealistic to say the least! But observing our thoughts is actually a really interesting practice, as it allows us to:

1. Learn how to detach from them.
2. Begin to see patterns and these habitual ways of thinking.

So, instead of emptying the mind, the key is to just observe. Why do we want to do this? Yogic philosophy explains that if we can become aware of patterns that may be tripping us up, and then reflect on them, we can discover the cause of those patterns, how they may have influenced us and how they may be keeping us from our goal of greater clarity.

This greater understanding of our past (purvajati jnanam) allows us to move forward to live more fully in the present—free from the compulsion to keep behaving in ways that cause us suffering and unhappiness or keep us small or stuck. One way to look at ourselves deeply is by taking a step back and observing our thoughts and the patterns that play out in them, rather than becoming them.

Through my own practice, I discovered that often, thoughts about things I wanted to do, whether big goals or small future plans, had a habitual thought pattern attached to them that went something like: 'That will never happen for me', or 'just my luck – it won't go well or be easy', or 'I don't deserve that'. I was setting myself up for failure in everything I was doing before I'd even done it by not believing I was deserving of my goal, or not 'good enough'. For years, most of my life in fact, I hadn't ever even realised that this story was playing on repeat every day in my thought patterns. But once I observed that I had this habitual way of thinking about myself and my goals, I was able to see that it was rooted in fear (*abhinivesha*).

This is a really powerful meditation; try and incorporate it into your practice at least three times a week if you can, in order to observe your thoughts, discover habitual patterns and begin to see where your thinking is holding you back. From there, we will reflect on this new wisdom within the Wheels of Wellfulness in order to begin to release ourselves and move forward.

one

Move to or create a 'sacred' space, where you won't be distracted and set a timer for anywhere between 5–10 minutes, or longer if you wish.

two

Rather than focusing on your breath or sounds, in this meditation just use the flowing of thoughts through your mind as your anchor. Allow a thought to come into your mind. Try to simply observe it, without getting attached to stories around it, or being swept up in it so that it becomes your reality. Can you take a step back and look at this thought, as if you are looking at it from a distance? It might help to look at it as if you were seeing it as a friend.

three

Apply a sense of unbiased curiosity to your thought. Try not to judge it, just look at it and then allow it to pass and the next thought to arrive. You might think of observing the coming and going of each thought as being like watching clouds drifting by. I like to imagine each thought as a balloon, which I look at as I hold it in my mind, before consciously letting it go and watching it drift up into the sky. Some people like to say, 'Hello thought' and 'Goodbye thought'. See what works for you.

four

Keep watching the thoughts from that place of observation as they come and you consciously let them go. Now and then you'll get caught up in a thought – you'll forget to let go of it and start drifting along with it. That's normal. When you realize this is happening, simply choose to let the thought go. Over time, you'll get caught up in your thoughts less and less. You might even start to have brief moments where your mind seems empty.

five

After each meditation, write down what you observed and any patterns you discovered. Remember to be non-judgemental. This is not an opportunity to be unkind to yourself. If you find yourself doing this, simply bring your awareness to it. Be curious about your unkindness - is this another pattern for you? Write down how this makes you feel.

Feel your feelings

Every morning, usually in the shower as it's away from any distraction, I like to check in with how I'm feeling. It's a great way to start the day and of getting to understand myself better – and it only takes moments. I simply close my eyes, bring my mind to my breath and ask myself, 'How do I feel?' Then I ask the same question again and then a third time to really focus my mind on it and start to explore my feelings in that exact moment – in my body, mind and heart. Essentially, I'm completing the first step of the Wheels of Wellfulness (see page 42) in my head for that specific, present experience.

Once I've have identified an emotion, I notice where it is in my body and try to look at it with unbiased curiosity, asking whether it is negative or positive. If it's negative, I ask if I can sit with it, looking at it without trying to push it away, distract myself or change it. If it's pleasant or positive, I ask if I can just be with it, let it be, without trying to embrace it in a deeper way. Once I have sat with the feeling for a few moments, I bring my attention back to my breath, then breathe in a sense of kindness and breathe out a sense of gratitude towards myself for taking the time to do this short meditation.

I've found this practice especially helpful when I'm experiencing a really uncomfortable or intense emotion. Often, in such moments, our feelings are so strong or extreme that we can't focus on anything else. A natural reaction to a powerful emotion is often to push it away, reject or try to ignore it, numbing it with something else, such as food, alcohol or even another emotion, just so we don't have to feel it any more. But this doesn't make it go away. In fact, it usually makes it more powerful.

Through mindfulness, however, we can discover that turning towards our emotions and simply looking at them, acknowledging them and allowing them to be there, actually makes them more bearable to deal with and often diminishes their power. When we look at them for a few moments and sit with them, without judgement but with compassion, then intense emotions usually stop shouting at us so loudly. This might take an element of acceptance, but it is not an acceptance in the sense that we allow ourselves to be ruled by this emotion. It is an active acceptance that this is the way things are, at least for now, in this moment.

Be conscious of shooting the second arrow

A Zen story that I love is of a monk walking through the forest. From afar, thinking the monk is a deer, an archer accidently aims his bow at the monk and shoots. The arrow hits the monk, piercing his skin and knocking him down. The archer rushes to the monk's side to find him in obvious pain, but despite the suffering caused by the initial blow, the monk persuasively asks the archer to shoot him again. The archer, being asked by a holy monk, reluctantly obliges and a second arrow pierces the monk's skin, causing even more pain.

It can be hard to understand why the monk would ask the archer to shoot him a second time. Why would he choose more pain and suffering? Yet we do this in our own lives almost every day.

I was having dinner with a friend recently, who was running a massive PR campaign for a big, prestigious brand. She got a call from her assistant telling her there had been an error on the campaign images that had been sent out. Understandably, she was flustered. She left the table and hurriedly set about fixing the problem. The situation wasn't ideal, but she'd fixed it as best as she could at that time. Like the monk in the story, she had been struck by her first 'arrow'.

But back at the table, she began to panic that her boss would take the campaign away from her because of the mistake and, if that happened, she would be so embarrassed. She needed the campaign to be successful to get the promotion she had her eye on. If she didn't get that promotion, then she wouldn't be able to move to a bigger house next year, and she and her husband needed more space, as they were planning to try for a baby soon. If she had to wait longer before trying for a baby, her grandmother, who was ill, might die without meeting her grandchild. The worst-case scenarios spiralled, whirls of 'what if' and 'what then' whipping up in my friend's mind. As I listened to her, I witnessed her shoot a second, third, fourth, fifth and then sixth 'arrow' at herself, causing herself more and more suffering. In mindfulness we call this secondary suffering. My friend's primary suffering was the initial situation that she couldn't change – the error in campaign images – but her secondary suffering was the reaction she had to it.

In the Zen story, the Buddha explains, 'In life, we cannot always control the first arrow. However, the second arrow is our reaction to the first. And with the second arrow comes the possibility of choice.' Think back to a situation when you might have got angry at yourself for some error or problem that had arisen and then let your mind fill with thoughts of all the catastrophes that might happen because of it. I can think of being told we had to move house with just a week's notice. I had so many commitments that week – work, appointments and meetings that needed my full attention. I had no idea how I would get all of it done and yet it all had to happen. I reacted by shooting a volley or 'arrows' at myself – 'My work will suffer. It will be a disaster! I should have been more organized. I'll never get it all done. I'm a failure…'

My heart started to beat faster, I began to sweat and felt claustrophobic. Anxiety quickly escalated to panic. I got angry and then I began to get upset. Mentally, I felt paralysed. I couldn't think, get my words out properly or come up with a plan as to how to get through it all.

Using mindfulness can help in such situations, but it doesn't always mean it will help you to deal immediately with every situation life throws at you. When all this emotional turmoil was whirling around in my mind, I seemed to forget all I'd ever learned about mindfulness. Later, once the initial panic had passed and the whirlpool of thoughts and reactions had settled enough for me to look at them and see them for the secondary suffering they were, I took myself to a place I knew would help me – acceptance.

We've talked about practising conscious acceptance in areas of our lives where we cannot change the things we wish we could. I had to move house, so there was no getting around that. This was my primary suffering and I couldn't change it. The only option I had, other than to fight it and cause myself more suffering, was to accept it. I didn't want to say, or couldn't say, no to the other commitments I had that week either, so I had to accept that too. Why had I panicked and given myself so much secondary suffering? Was it fear that I wouldn't get it all done? Was it resentment for having to do it all so quickly? What had stopped me from accepting my situation?

'Conditions' of the mind

People have documented the things they have struggled with and ideas to help combat them for thousands of years, writing them down to pass on and help others. Reading yogic texts makes me realize that I'm not alone with my suffering and, being reminded of that, is a huge part of Mindfulness – finding compassion for ourselves and others. However big or small the things are that cause the whirlpools of emotion in our minds, whatever we are feeling is part of being human and has been felt by millions of people before us. The ancient yogis theorized that every thought that causes us pain or discomfort, is rooted in one of the five 'kleshas', thought of as 'conditions of the mind that prevent us from being happy'. They are:

1. AVIDYA

A lack of perspective or clarity. This is the inability to see things as they truly are, or thinking something is true when it may not be. It is when we fail to really observe and therefore do not understand. If we can work on this klesha, we have the potential to remove all the others.

2. ASMITA

This is the tendency to overidentify with our ego. It might play out as expecting more of ourselves than is realistically possible. It makes it difficult for us to accept situations and forgive or feel compassion for both ourselves and others.

3. RAGA

This is when we develop an unhealthy attachment to our desires, rather then being satisfied with what we have. It also involves a need for perfection.

4. DVESHA

This involves pushing away painful or uncomfortable feelings or situations, which can stop us from learning about ourselves and suffocate our growth. It is also the rejection of things we do not understand or are unfamiliar with.

5. ABHINIVESHA

This the fear of change and our inability to control situations in our lives, and not trusting that everything will be okay. Ultimately, all fear boils down to a fear of death.

MIND

Each klesha generates thoughts that lead to patterns of behaviour, which become embedded in your mind. Do you have a repetitive thought that torments you? A common one is 'I'm not good enough.' Or, do you have a habitual and damaging way of dealing with situations, such as being very controlling or avoiding confrontation? These patterns of behaviour will have roots in one or more of the kleshas. Once you shine a light on them and observe them for what they are, you begin to understand them. If you put them through the Wheels of Wellfulness (see page 42), you will almost always discover that they do not serve you and from there gain perspective, which is the key to starting to let your damaging behaviour and suffering go.

You may remember that in the chapter on space I wrote about repetitive patterns of behaviour that caused me a lot of pain, from being bullied, excluded and ignored. Once I understood that I had a habitual pattern of avoidance of confrontation in these situations, I began to see the part I played in my own suffering, and I saw the 'arrows' of pain I had shot at myself for years.

These secondary 'arrows' all came from the places where kleshas played out in my life. *Dvesha* was present in my life in my withdrawal from social situations and avoidance of simply confronting the cruel behaviour, and instead hiding from it. *Abhinivesha* also played a big part in my fear of implementing healthy boundaries. This lead to *asmita*, which made me feel as if the bullying was my fault and not see that the hurt did not start with me, but was projected onto me by others because of their pain. My ego held on to a victim mindset I had come to feel so comfortable with.

Realizing my own role in these hurtful situations didn't take the pain of being excluded, ignored and rejected away. I could not and will never be able to control how people treat me. But I learned that I could control how much secondary suffering I placed on myself. Ultimately, the ongoing pain attached to other people's actions only existed if I allowed it to.

YOU ARE THE ANSWER

Joseph Campbell, author and Professor of Literature at Stanford, did a great deal of work around the recurring patterns in the narratives that play out in most mythology (often referred to as 'the hero's journey'). He wrote: 'Life has no meaning. Each of us has meaning and we bring it to life. It is a waste to be asking the question when you are the answer.' I love this idea, because it stops us from looking for meaning outside of ourselves, and asks us to look inside. It empowers us to discover and pull out the answers that are within us, to consult our inner wisdom, follow our own inner north star, and apply our own version of meaning to our lives. This is a place to empower ourselves to live to our fullest potential. To love more, to be more conscious, to live to our values more – to take control and live the life we want to live.

Applying Wellfulness to your mind might seem a more daunting task than applying it to other elements in your life. But it doesn't need to be. Ultimately, the aim of mindfulness is to allow you, through awareness, to find the space to pause and respond rather than just mindlessly react, which can create situations that don't serve you. Equally, however, uncovering these reactions can help recognize thought patterns and beliefs that don't nourish or help you. So let's practise becoming more enlightened and shine a light on those secondary, reactional 'arrows' you may shoot at yourself, so that you can begin to unpick the patterns and free yourself from mindless suffering:

one

Think of a difficult situation you were recently in. It might be an argument with your partner because they accused you of being selfish, or a bout of road rage after another driver cuts you up, or becoming anxious because a delayed train is making you late for work. On a scale of 1 to 10, with 10 being very difficult, choose a situation that feels around 5 on the scale.

two

Draw or print a Wheels of Wellfulness diagram. Identify what triggered your difficult situation. Note that the trigger, or primary 'arrow' is the part of the situation that you cannot change.

three

Try and remember the thoughts you attached to this primary 'arrow'. Ask yourself how these thoughts make, or

made, you feel in your mind, in your heart and in your body – really try and feel the effect they had on you physically and emotionally and even how they triggered even more thoughts – and write all of this down on your Wheels of Wellfulness diagram.

four

Now think about the reactions or behaviour that resulted from your situation. Ask how these make, or made, you feel in mind, body and heart. Enter the answers on your Wheels of Wellfulness diagram. You will now have a picture of all the secondary 'arrows' attached to your situation and how they made you feel.

five

Take a look at your completed Wheels of Wellfulness. Can you see any patterns – any ways in which your thoughts and actions could be attached to any of the kleshas (see page 182).

six

Now ask yourself, in body, mind and heart, which of your thoughts and actions served you and which didn't. Enter all of this in the intersections of a fresh Wheels of Wellfulness diagram. Do any of your thoughts and actions make their way into the golden, inner nucleus of Wellfulness? What is your Wheels of Wellfulness telling you? What do you need?

seven

When doing this activity, always remember that it's important to apply acceptance towards yourself. It's okay to acknowledge any emotions you're starting to attach to the thoughts and behaviour that surfaced in reaction to your situation, or primary 'arrow'. All your secondary 'arrows', or reactions, were most likely your way of trying to deal with or fix a situation that couldn't be changed. They are in the past, so let them go. Also, can you practise some acceptance around the initial situation? Send some compassionate acceptance towards yourself now. This allows you to let go of the need to place further suffering upon yourself. It also allows you to find clarity around your suffering and consider that it might stem from a specific kleshas?

eight

Once you've absorbed all of this, ask yourself, 'What can I consciously change? What do I want to let go of? What do I want to do more of? What do I need to consciously change or transform, in order to respond to and accept a difficult situation, rather than react to it and cause more self-inflicted suffering?' Be specific, make a plan and don't forget that everything is best served with a good splash of self-compassion.

The empowerment of choice

When we react to situations in our lives, we operate from a place of unconscious autopilot, rather than from a place of mindful awareness, and so we shut the door on the most important thing we are aiming to cultivate through The Wellfulnness Project – choice. It is only when we become aware we have choice that we can begin to respond to our situations instead of reacting to them, and so bring conscious and transformative change into our lives.

There is so much empowerment in remembering you have a choice. When you bring mindful awareness to the situations you have to navigate in life, you realize that you almost always have choice, even if you don't really like any of the options you're presented with. Back in the chapter on body and movement, I mentioned that for so long exercise was something I forced myself to do. It felt like punishment. I dreaded it and resented it. Such negative energy existed in that relationship with my body. Every day was a battle in which I'd react to my perceived lack of options – not exercise and feel guilty or torture myself with exercise! Both involved unkindness and punishment.

When I looked a little closer and listened a little deeper, I discovered that in my heart I did value a healthy body. Being fit allows me to do the things I want to do – run around after my niece, feel comfortable on the beach and even limit my chances of serious illness. All those things make me feel great and enhance my life. When I reconnected with my values around what was important to me, exercise became something that I accepted as necessary to me. This is the wisdom that I now strive to listen to within myself. It is the inner wisdom, not to be found in the surface chitter-chatter of my consciousness, but an innate elemental part of who I am and what I believe and value.

Some of the things you want to achieve in life will involve hard work or what you might perceive as sacrifice, so that they become fertile ground for creating secondary suffering. But by practising acceptance of the situation, and compassion to yourself within it, it becomes easier to stop fighting and relinquish the struggle against your sacrifices. I now find myself consciously and powerfully choosing to do the things I once pushed away and am opting for choices I would have once fought against, because ultimately I am choosing to love myself enough to do the work for the things I want. And oh, how freeing it is to end the war against myself and choose, every day, to love myself!

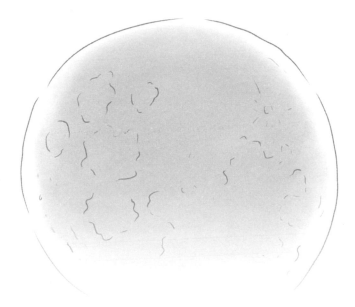

Mind Closing Ritual

This closing ritual will help you to find clarity around what supports, serves and nourishes your mental health, and what disserves it, so that you are empowered to let go of the habitual thought processes or practices that don't support you, and cultivate more of that which does. At the end, you'll have a complete and unique Wellfulness Plan for your mental health. Find a safe and sacred space, grab your journal or print out a WoW template and smile – this is where huge growth is to be found.

one

Begin by taking a small breathing-space meditation. Close your eyes and inhale. deeply to the count of 4, then hold your breath to the count of 4, then exhale to the count of four. Pause briefly and repeat for 3–5 breath cycles. Open your eyes.

two

Bring your focus to all of the things, practices, people that support your mental health; meditation, walking in nature, your therapist? Now bring to mind the things that you do which don't serve you; spending too long on social media, shooting secondary arrows at yourself. Focus on how each one makes you feel, rather than the stories and judgements you may attach to them. Simply observe the feelings.

three

Now consider how each one makes you feel: body, mind and heart? How does it serve you? How does it nourish you? Find the joy here! Be curious and playful. Enter each one into the relevant circles, or intersections if they overlap by serving two, or even all three areas of body, mind and heart for you (see an example on page 193).

four

Now ask: 'What's not serving me?' What doesn't nourish or serve your body, mind and heart? Place these outside your Wheels of Wellfulness, as I have in the example. Try not to judge these as 'negative', or find ways to change them. Just notice that they exist, and bring those that aren't serving you to mind with a sense of kindness and compassion.

five

Now look at the contents of each circle for body, mind and heart. Everything in the middle intersection where all three wheels overlap, are the things that serve you fully on a holistic level. Everything outside your wheels are the things that do not serve you. The things that sit within one wheel, are only serving you on a very basic level, and it's your choice as to whether you continue or adapt them to suit you on a more holistic level. The things outside your wheels completely do not serve you, and with this new awareness, you can decide whether accept them, let them go, or adapt them to they meet your needs. This completed Wheel of Wellfulness is your Mind Wellness Plan. Keep it safe – you'll be using it to complete an all-encompassing unique-to-you Wellfulness Plan at the end of the book.

six

It's time to consider the next steps you'll take through conscious acceptance and conscious change. Ask yourself, or journal your answers to the questions below:

- Is there anything you need to practice compassionate acceptance around your discoveries? For example, the fact that you are very liberal with shooting secondary arrows at yourself. You might want to practise acceptance that you've been doing this unknowingly, until now, with a sense of kindness towards yourself?

- Now, looking at your wheels, what will you consciously change? For example, acupuncture really helped your stress levels last year, so you're going to book a monthly top-up session. Or making a conscious effort to stop gossiping because it doesn't sit well in your heart.

- If you feel any resistance to the idea of accepting or changing, simply observe these thoughts and bring back a sense of conscious compassionate acceptance. Can you allow yourself to just observe this resistance and allow it to be? What's that like?

seven

So, taking this all into account, how will you continue to cultivate conscious choices when it comes to your mental health? What new practises will you create? What isn't serving you that you are going to let go of? Get curious, and get excited – you're making huge changes to create a happier, healthier mind.

What's not serving me?

BODY

Too little sleep

MIND

Overthinking

———

Shooting myself with the second arrow

———

Catastrophizing

———

Looking for the threats/negatives

HEART

Overworking and little rest

———

Living my life from the kleshas; ignorance, ego, desire, avoidance, fear

———

Gossiping

BODY

MIND

HEART

Mindfulness
meditations
————
Dharma talks
————
Being in nature
————
Hatha yoga
————
Acupuncture
————
Calming breathing
practices/pranayama

Acceptance practices
————
Locating where an
emotion lives in
my body

Studying yogic and
buddhist texts and
philosophies
————
Reading psychological
experiments
————
Therapy

Gratitude diary
————
Journalling
————
Remembering
I have a voice

Wheels of Wellfulness: my unique Wellfulness plan for my daily mind

Part Four
A Life of Wellfulness

'Listen – are you breathing just a little,
and calling it a life?'

– Mary Oliver

PUTTING IT ALL TOGETHER

Studies in wellness science suggest that when we create a combination of good physical health, emotional balance and positive social connections within our environment, we can create a self-sustaining, upward-spiral dynamic wherein each element supports and enhances the other, creating greater wellbeing in our lives. Over the course of this book, we've worked with love on all three of these elements.

You've dedicated time to thinking about each one, bringing your golden light of awareness to them, looking within and getting well and truly in touch with that inner wisdom. You've considered what it is you need in order to create more harmony in your holistic health, and support your own unique needs in body, mind and heart.

By now you should have a folder or journal full of Wheels of Wellfulness diagrams; small maps of your unique wellbeing wisdom, from food, to exercise, environment, people, habits, and the way you deal with difficult situations. This is your blueprint for a specific and exclusive-to-you wellness plan.
The most exciting part for me, is that no one, no expert or psychologist, or dietician, or personal trainer or yoga teacher, or energy healer, can create this for you. It is made by you, for you; a love letter of commitment and dedication to living a more conscious, free and full life. Is there anything more beautiful? Take a moment to appreciate that and all that you have invested in yourself.

I see my own Wellfulness practice as an enormous act of self-love and dedication to my health and happiness. And that's something I am truly grateful for, and proud of. Completing this book and living a life of Wellfulness is a truly courageous, spirited thing to embark on, and shining the light of awareness onto the way we live our lives is continuously life changing.

A Final Ritual

Bring your five main Wellfulness Plan wheels from the closing ritual of each section; food, body, space, ritual and mind. These are going to look different for each and every one of us. We interpret the concepts in these life areas in many different ways, and each one will have different levels of meaning and importance for all of us. There is no right or wrong, only uniqueness, and that is something to be celebrated!

So, grab your favourite mug of something hot, wrap yourself in your cosiest blanket and gather yourself and all of your Wellfulness Plans to your sacred space. From these plans, together we'll create your unique holistic Wellfulness Plan: one all-encompassing, detailed wellness map that includes every area of your life: food, body, space, ritual, mind, in one place. Yours to keep forever.

one

Work through your Wellfulness Plans for each chapter: food, body, space, ritual and mind to pull out the practices, habits, rituals, spaces, foods, exercises, times, routines, people, thought patterns, meditations, and anything and everything else you've discovered, that serve, nourish and work for you. You will now enter them into a large Wheels of Wellfulness diargram as before, but this time, collecting them all together in one place.

two

First, take the practices that appear in the inner 'holistic heart' intersection of each Wellfulness Plan you've created – the ones that serve you in all three elements of body, mind and heart. Add them to this all-encompassing wheel so that you can see them all together.

three

Then add all the practices that sit in the outer intersections – the ones that only serve two of the elements of body, mind and heart.

four

Now add anything that only serves one element of body, mind or heart – these will sit inside the corresponding, ring but not within the intersections of the rings.

five

And finally, add anything that doesn't serve you at all, outside the three circles altogether.

six

You now have your full Wellfulness Plan – an all-encompassing view of everything that serves you, and doesn't serve you, in your life in one place – a map of wellness, uniquely designed for you, by you.

Once you've finished, take a step back and look at your plan. You should have a map of all areas of your life and the practices that serve and nourish your holistic health that you have consciously decide to keep, build on or enhance, and the ones that you are ready to let go of that don't serve you or even damage your holistic health. You might want to do this on a computer so that you have a digital version you can carry around on your phone, or edit as time passes.

Remember, your Wellfulness Plan is not fixed. If I've offered one truth in this book, it is that life is ever changing and fluid – and so are you. Your internal and external circumstances will change, new health practices and trends will arrive that you might want to try, and you will change – your needs, your passions, who you are. And so, as life moves forwards, so will your Wellfulness Plan. And it is my hope that you will consciously move it forwards, adjust, amend and transform it to suit you, with every change that occurs, every new circumstance, every new practice you try, so that you know in your bones that it serves and nourishes you and has a place in your life.

This conscious Wellfulness Plan you've created is just your first version. I hope you'll continuously tweak it to suit you more fully as often as you need to, just as I do. Wellfulness is a lifelong practice of self-care. It's a ritual that I hope serves you and allows you to live more consciously and therefore more authentically. I wrote a few pages back that, ultimately, we all just want to be happy. And I believe that taking steps to live more authentically, with ourselves, our needs and our values, to choose the life that uniquely serves us, to fill it with the things that nourish us, is a sure step towards creating a fuller, freer, and more Wellful life.

What's not serving me?

BODY

Too much junk food

———

Physical clutter

———

Too little sleep

MIND

Overthinking

———

Shooting myself with
the second arrow

———

Catastrophizing

———

Looking for the
threats/negatives

———

Looking for the
threats/negatives

HEART

Overworking and
little rest

———

Living my life
from the kleshas;
ignorance, ego, desire,
avoidance, fear

———

Checking emails
at the weekend

———

Gossiping

BODY

MIND

HEART

High protein and
high fat foods

Gentle yoga and
swimming when I'm
feeling fatigued

Meditations

Acceptance practices

Being in nature

Locating where an
emotion lives in
my body

Organising
tomorrow's
bag before
dinner

Morning movement

Acupuncture

Unconditional love/
Friends/Family

Studying yogic and
Buddhist texts and
philosophies

Sprints and spin

Sentimental or
meaningful
jewellery

Pets

Trying new recipes

Gratitude diary

Sustainably
packaged foods

Remembering
I have choice

Wheels of Wellfulness: my unique holistic Wellfulness plan

Bibliography

Algoe, S B; Brantley, M; Catalino L I; Coffey K A; Cohn, M A; Fredrickson, B L; Kok, B E; Vacharkulksemsuk, T: 'How positive emotions build physical health: perceived positive social connections account for the upward spiral between positive emotions and vagal tone' (*Psychological Science*, 2016)

Ando, S; Ebara, S; Ishii, Y; Matsui, T; Sawamura, H; Watanabe T; Yuasa, M I: 'Consumption of a low-carbohydrate and high-fat diet (the ketogenic diet) exaggerates biotin deficiency in mice' (*Nutrition*, 2013)

Balkrishna, A; Kumar, N; Sharma, S; Telles, S; Visweshwaraiah, N K; Yadav, A: 'Blood pressure and Purdue pegboard scores in individuals with hypertension after alternate nostril breathing, breath awareness, and no intervention' (*Medical Science Monitor: International Medical Journal of Experimental and Clinical Research*, 2013)

Balsters, J H; Dockree, P M; Melnychuk, M C; Murphy, P R; O'Connell, R G; Robertson, I H: Coupling of respiration and attention via the locus coeruleus: effects of meditation and pranayama' (*Psychophysiology*, 2018)

Barrett, M S; Cucchiara, A J; Gooneratne, N S; Sharma, A; Thase, M E: 'A breathing-based meditation intervention for patients with major depressive disorder following inadequate response to antidepressants' (*The Journal of Clinical Psychiatry*, 2016)

Beck, A: 'The past and the future of cognitive therapy' (*Journal of Psychotherapy Practice and Research*; 6, 276-284,1997)

Bhuvaneswari, T; Kumar, R A; Ramaprabha, P: 'Effect of Nadi Shodana pranayama on cardiovascular parameters among first-year MBBS students' (*International Research Journal of Pharmaceutical and Applied Sciences*, 2013)

Birch, K; Mason, H (eds.): Yoga For Mental Health (*Handspring Publishing*, 2018)

Boden-Albala, B; Gangwisch, J E; Heymsfield, S; Malaspina, D: 'Inadequate sleep as a risk factor for obesity: analyses of the NHANES I' (*Sleep*, 2005)

Brown, K W; Creswell, J D; Lindsay, E K; Pacilio, L E: 'Brief mindfulness meditation training alters psychological and neuroendocrine responses to social evaluative stress' (*Psychoneuroendocrinology*, 2014)

Brown, R P; Gerberg, P L: 'Sudarshan Kriya yogic breathing in the treatment of stress, anxiety, and depression: Part II—clinical applications and guidelines', (*The Journal of Alternative and Complementary Medicine*, 2005)

Buchwald, D; Goldberg, J; Harden, K P; Pack, A I; Strachan, E; Vitiello, M V; Watson, N F: 'Sleep duration and depressive symptoms: a gene-environment interaction' (*Sleep*, 2014)

Carlson, E N: 'Overcoming the barriers to self-knowledge: Mindfulness as a path to seeing yourself as you really are (*Perspectives on Psychological Science*, 2013)

Carmod, J; Congleton, C; Gard, T; Hölzel, B K; Lazar, S W; Vange, M; Yerramsetti, S M: 'Mindfulness practice leads to increases in regional brain gray matter density' (*Psychiatry Research: Neuroimaging*, 2011)

Chi, D S; Kasasbeh, E; Krishnaswamy G: 'Inflammatory aspects of sleep apnea and their cardiovascular consequences' (*Southern Medical Journal*, 2006)

Craig, A D: 'How do you feel – now? The anterior insula and human awareness' (*Nature*, 2009)

Decety, J; Moriguchi, Y: 'The empathic brain and its dysfunction in psychiatric populations: implications for intervention across different clinical conditions' (*Biopsychosocial Medicine*, 2007)

Eisen, A; Mor, N; Perl, O; Ravia, A; Rubinson, M; Secundo, L; Soroka, T: 'Human non-olfactory cognition phase-locked with inhalation.' (*Nature*, 2019)

Esch, T; Stefano, G B: 'The neurobiological link between compassion and love' (*Medical Science Monitor: International Medical Journal of Experimental and Clinical Research*, 17(3), RA65-75, 2011)

Farb, N; Mehling, W E: 'Interoception, contemplative practice and health' (*Frontiers in Psychology*, 2016)

Ferreiro, F; Senra, C; Seoane, G: 'Toward understanding the role of body dissatisfaction in the gender differences in depressive symptoms and disordered eating: a longitudinal study during adolescence' (*Journal of Adolescence*; 37(1): 73–84, 2014)

Foster, G D; Hill, J O; Wyatt, H R et al: 'Weight and metabolic outcomes after two years on a low-carbohydrate versus low-fat diet – a randomized trial' (*Ann Intern Med*;153(3):147-57, 2010)

Gouin, J; Hantsoo, L; Kiecolt-Glaser, J (eds.): 'Stress, negative emotions, and inflammation' (*The Oxford Handbook of Social Neuroscience*, 2011)

Kalyani, B G et al: 'Neurohemodynamic correlates of 'OM' chanting A pilot functional magnetic resonance imaging study' (*International Journal of Yoga*, 2011)

Kastner, S; McMains, S I: 'Interactions of top-down and bottom-up mechanisms in human visual cortex' (*The Journal of Neuroscience*, 2011)

Langevin, H M; Yandow, J A: 'Relationship of acupuncture points and meridians to connective tissue planes' (*The Anatomical Record* (New Anat.) 269: 257–265, 2002)

Rahinel, R; Redden, J P; Vohs, K D: 'Physical order produces healthy choices, generosity, and conventionality, whereas disorder produces creativity' (*Psychological Science*, 2013)

About the Author

Ali is editor-at-large and a columnist at *Psychologies Magazine*, where she has interviewed world-renowned spiritual gurus and wise women and men, including Deepak Chopra, Gabrielle Bernstein, Byron Katie, Jon Kabat-Zinn and Mastin Kipp. Her work at *Psychologies Magazine* has changed her life, prompting her to explore deeper within herself to find contentment and wellness in body and mind. Ali holds a BSc (Hons) degree in Psychology, and will shortly qualify as a Mindfulness for Stress teacher and expert at the highly esteemed facility Breathworks. She is a qualified '200hr Yoga Alliance Certified' teacher, and is passionate about combining Western sciences of psychology, neuroscience and coaching with the Eastern philosophies of meditation, mindfulness and yoga, to cultivate true happiness and wellbeing. She is also co-founder of the yoga and mindfulness retreat and brunch company The Remedy Retreats with her husband, which launched in 2018.

Connect with Ali:

 @AliRoff
 @AliRoff
www.aliroff.com

You can download a version of the Wheels of Wellfulness at Ali's website www.aliroff.com for both your individual practices and your master plans.

Acknowledgements

To my teachers; my friend 'the naughty monk' Tim Steel for your weekly wisdom and playful energy – you lead me to think deeper each week, and have inspired me with confidence to do the things I never thought possible in my practice, which has poured over into the rest of my life and my own teachings. You are a special soul. Beautiful Avani of Om Cashew Hill and the tribe of women she brings together, who, though scattered across the world, I will always be connected to. And Ginny and the wise and wonderful Breathworks team who have guided me on my journey to be able to teach all that I know of mindfulness.

Thank you to my glorious agent Valeria who believed in my voice before the idea for this book even existed. Your championing, support and friendship mean more than you know.

Thank you to Stephanie at Octopus for your sheer belief in me, for grabbing my hands with so much enthusiasm that it lifted me off my feet back in June 2018, and inviting me to write this book. It has been a dream come true, and I am so happy to be a part of such an innovative publishing family at Octopus. I'm still floating.

And of course, lovely Sophie for your kindness, support and perspective along the editing process, and brilliant Yasia for creating a book that is so visually beautiful. Thank you for inviting and adopting my ideas, and bringing your own genius to create something so uniquely beautiful.

Thank you to the warrior women of *Psychologies Magazine* – for always walking our talk, for your creativity and wisdom, and especially Suzy who I have learnt so much from and miss sitting next to, soaking in your wisdom and energy each day. Thank you for always supporting me.

To my friends who allow me to be me, who champion, who love openly, who understood my disappearing to write this book for months on end and welcomed me back when I resurfaced, only with love.

To my family. My parents, who taught me the kindness and ineffable love which is the thread that holds these pages together, and is at the core of everything I hope to share with this world.

My sister, with whom I have shared so much of this book and the ideas in it in so many ways. We are one, always.

And my husband, who dreams with me daily. Thank you for selflessly providing me the space to write this book. For always believing with me that something wonderful is about to happen. For holding me up, for loving me. Unconditionally.

Index